Stepping
Back
from the
Ledge

Stepping Back from the Ledge

A Daughter's Search for Truth and Renewal

Laura Trujillo

RANDOM HOUSE · NEW YORK

Published in the United States by Random House,
an imprint and division of Penguin Random House LLC, New York.

RANDOM HOUSE and the HOUSE colophon are registered trademarks
of Penguin Random House LLC.

LIBRARY OF CONGRESS CATALOGING-IN-PUBLICATION DATA

Names: Trujillo, Laura, author.
Title: Stepping back from the ledge : a daughter's search for truth and renewal /
Laura Trujillo.
Description: First edition. | New York : Random House, [2022] | Includes
bibliographical references.
Identifiers: LCCN 2021006621 (print) | LCCN 2021006622 (ebook) |
ISBN 9780593157619 (hardcover) | ISBN 9780593157626 (ebook)
Subjects: LCSH: Trujillo, Laura. | Children of suicide victims—United States—
Biography. | Sexually abused teenagers—United States—Biography. | Mothers and
daughters—United States—Biography.
Classification: LCC HV6545 .T78 2022 (print) | LCC HV6545 (ebook) |
DDC 362.28/3092 [B]—dc23
LC record available at https://lccn.loc.gov/2021006621
LC ebook record available at https://lccn.loc.gov/2021006622

randomhousebooks.com

2 4 6 8 9 7 5 3 1

Printed in Canada

First Edition

Book design by Diane Hobbing

For Henry, Theo, Luke, and Lucy

Contents

Stepping Back from the Ledge

Chapter 1

Searching for Answers

I STOOD AND looked down into the canyon, at a spot where millions of years ago, a river cut through stone. Everything about the view is awe-inspiring and impossible, a landscape that seems to defy both physics and description. It is a view in a place that dwarfs you, that magnifies the questions in your mind about your place in the world and about the world itself, and that keeps the answers to itself.

It was April 26, 2016—four years since my mom died. Four years to the day since she stood in this same spot and looked out at this same view. I caught my breath here, and felt dizzy and needed to remind myself to breathe in through my nose and out through my mouth, slower, and again. I could say it out loud now: This is where my mom killed herself. She jumped from the edge of the Grand Canyon. From the edge of the earth.

I had come back to the spot because, finally, I was ready— I wanted to know everything. Like a lot of people who lose someone they love to suicide, I had been shocked. Numb.

Now I wanted to understand how this could have happened and what I could have done differently, what we all might have done differently to help her. What could have caused this? Was there a tipping point?

My eyes followed a narrow trail down, cutting through layers of red and purple rock that felt as if it were another planet, until the trail disappeared into a patch of green.

I'd been at this spot before, with my mother. My mom brought me here once when I was a child, and we'd walked along the rocky South Rim. She brought me here again when I was in college, this time for a mother-daughter trip where we exhausted ourselves hiking the 7.1 miles down to the canyon's floor and slept in a cabin: We spent more time together just the two of us than we ever would again. In between, my mom hiked more than a dozen trails at the canyon, finding a sense of adventure and strength, of peace and spirituality. She had watched the sunrise at Easter Mass here and had sat along the edge at night when the canyon disappears into a hole of black, with only the stars visible. For her, it was a place where she rediscovered herself after her divorce from my father, and later where she went to escape the world.

Now, I didn't just want to know everything. I needed to know it: the latitude and longitude where she fell, the last words she said to the shuttle bus driver who dropped her at the trail overlook, her mood when she met with her priest just four days prior. He had told me my mom went out of her way to say she was good, but he had sensed she was hiding something. I had tracked all of this down to try to piece it together, my mother's life.

I read over the last letter she had mailed to my children. I looked for clues inside that little card with a cartoon penguin drawn on the front: She wrote in block printing so my five-year-old daughter, Lucy, could read it easily. My mom wrote of riding the light rail to a Diamondbacks baseball game in Phoenix, of planting a cactus garden, of looking forward to summer in the already hot days of spring in the desert.

I also read and re-read her last words, written in cursive in the tiniest composition book, which she had left in her Jeep, as well as the last text she typed, in which she both celebrated life and apologized for it: "Life. My life has been such a gift. I'm so very sorry to disappoint all of you. In my heart I know this is not right but it's all I can do. Please pray for my soul."

I zoomed in on the photo she took with her iPhone from the ledge, the photo looking out to the sunrise that lit the canyon on that morning. I wanted to see if the rocks or shadows would reveal anything new. I re-played our last conversation in my mind, and each one before that, and before that, all of them I could remember. None of them seemed to have given any hints of what was to come. I last heard her voice on Easter, which on that year was also my birthday, talking about my children and chocolate bunnies, the irises blooming in our neighbors' yard, and when she might be able to visit. The conversation ended like thousands before it. I said, "I love you, Mom," and she said, "Love you, kiddo."

I wanted to know every fact, every detail, to see everything she saw, because I didn't have the one thing I wanted— the why. Now, I wondered why we didn't see it coming somehow, why we didn't do more, when it all seemed so clear. Looking back over the years, there were signs of depression and sadness, anxiety and regret, but sometimes we didn't really see, and we were silent about so many things.

I came back to the canyon for answers, or a deeper understanding of life and my mom, of her secrets and mine. But all I could see were the peaks miles away, the trees greener and prettier than I imagined, tiny dots of figures moving slowly up the switchbacks, and the stillness of the world.

I'd been told that suicide is as common and unknowable as the wind that shaped this rock. It's unspeakable, bewildering, confounding, devastating, sad. Don't try to figure it out, I had told myself; stop asking questions, assigning blame, looking. Yet I went on trying. How could I not? Now here I stood, looking, searching, suppressing the urge I had to follow her.

The morning she died, she tried to reach me. I saw "Mom" pop up on my phone shortly after ten A.M. I was at my desk on the nineteenth floor of *The Cincinnati Enquirer* building, working at a new job as the managing editor of the newsroom. I hadn't quite settled in to my role yet—there was just one photo of my children on my desk. I sat in the middle of an open office, at a desk between the receptionist and one of the digital news producers, a space where privacy was difficult to find.

I declined the call, and quickly texted: "I love you, Mom. Crazy busy workday. Hard to break away to talk. But know I love you." I had just walked out of one news meeting and sat down for a minute before the next one, trying to edit a sports story in the time between, while worrying about how my four children were adjusting to their new schools and making friends, and whether my husband had agreed to be home by five-thirty that night to start dinner, or I had. The rest of the day was a blur of talking through ideas with reporters and editors, eating a peanut butter sandwich at my desk, reading columns, and analyzing which stories were doing well online.

On my short drive home that night, I noticed the irises were starting to bloom in our neighborhood and I smiled and stopped the car, hopped out and took a photo of a deep purple iris to text to my mom. It was our favorite flower— hers because of the tenacity irises need to grow in the dry, rocky mountainside where she lived in Phoenix, and mine because when I was a kid, the irises always bloomed in early April, signaling it was almost time for my birthday. As I took the photo, I realized it was me who said I would be home that night, meaning I was already late. I would send the photo later; it could wait.

My parents divorced when I was eleven, and my father moved just a few miles away from us in Phoenix. We had stayed close through weekend visits, Wednesday-night dinners that almost always included a stop at an arcade to play Pac-Man, and softball games where he was my coach. I have my dad's Mexican American olive skin and his eyes that are so dark they are almost black, his look when I was little of quiet disdain for any number of transgressions that I now share with him when I am angry, and things like his need for buttered popcorn at the movies.

It was about five years after my dad left when my mom and I moved in with her boyfriend; she would marry him three years later. It was then that one of the corrosive secrets of my life and the life of my family began. The sexual abuse

I silenced, the dark stealth entry of my stepfather into my room at night, and how I believe my mom never knew. It was the secret I never told her.

Later, when I was an adult, my mom and I lived 3.3 miles away from each other. Sometimes she would stop on her way home from work to see my kids, and we would rub each other's hands while we sat on the short wood fence separating our yard from the neighbors' and talk about the day. Later, when she retired from her job as a hospital administrator, she often came by during the day when I was at work and the kids were home with the nanny. She would drive one of my children to play on the slides at the park, and then return to our house to stay late to read books or do puzzles with the family while I made dinner. When I moved from Phoenix to Ohio for a new job and to be closer to my husband's family, my mom and I talked on the phone every day. She was always up so early that even with the three-hour time difference, I could call her on my drive to work, sometimes describing the curve of the Ohio River as I drove along it, the way you would often see a barge, and how the trees were most beautiful in the winter because you could see their true shapes without the leaves. It felt as if she were a passenger in my car on my way to work, seeing what I saw along with me. We could make each other laugh, and sometimes it seemed that whatever she felt, I did, too.

That night, when I got home to the too expensive house we rented in Ohio, my husband, John, said he needed to talk to me. From his face, I could tell it was important. He said, "Come upstairs, and let's sit down."

I dropped my laptop in the entryway and put a lasagna in

the oven and started walking up the stairs, thinking about how I was home late from work, something that had happened too often recently. I figured he wasn't happy. We'd been arguing. We had moved from my hometown of Phoenix to Cincinnati three months earlier, and it had been a rough transition—a rental house while we hoped to find a house to buy, a new city where we had no family, four kids in new schools, and we seemed to be saying too often about bills, "Can you wait until next Friday?" Was I trying hard enough to make it work?

I kicked off my heels and sat down on the guest bed upstairs, pulling my knees up close to my chin, wrapping my arms around them.

John did not look angry. He looked serious. He was practical and to the point. He wasted no time.

"It's your mom," he said. "She's gone. She was at the Grand Canyon. They found her body in the canyon."

I realized he used the word *body*.

I couldn't think, couldn't process order or time, yet I had to move, to do something. I took John's T-shirts out of a drawer and mindlessly began to re-fold them. I had too many feelings to control or even understand; I couldn't find something to say. There was a pain that made my bones feel like noodles. I walked into the guest bathroom and knelt down on the tile.

I began to cry in a way that sounded like a wounded animal.

"This is my fault," I said. I stretched my arms out to the floor, almost like the child's pose in yoga, thinking it would help me breathe. "I did this," I said, "I did this."

John walked over to me and knelt down.

"Oh, Laura Kay," he said, using my middle name that he uses when he is being sweet.

He sat down next to me on the floor, leaning against the bathroom vanity, his hand on my head. He told me what he knew about my mom's death—my older sister had called him with the details so that he could tell me in person. I felt if I didn't force myself to get up, I might remain there on the floor forever, crying and trying to catch my breath, trying to breathe through the sobbing. John stood up first, took my hands, and helped pull me up. He wrapped me into a hug.

"We need to tell the kids," I finally said, trying to move into devising a plan. My mind almost went into Excel spreadsheet mode, trying to find a sense of calm by asserting order and creating tasks. I needed to talk to the kids. I couldn't work the next day. Someone needed to alert my boss. I needed to figure out which projects were left unfinished in the office. Did anyone have baseball practice that night? I needed to start looking at plane tickets to go home to Phoenix, I needed to figure out how much school the kids could miss. We were supposed to go to Chicago that weekend, and now I was rearranging weekend plans in my head, that we needed to call my mother-in-law and let her know, and the boys would be home for their weekend games, and we should call the coach.

"Slow down," John said. "One thing now, one thing later."

Before we went downstairs, John called one of our new friends in Cincinnati who happened to be a child neuropsychologist, and his wife, a family counselor. Their daughter was good friends with our youngest, but they also had come to know our other three children. Our friends joined the call together, and John briefly recounted what had happened and asked for advice on how we should tell the children.

"Be honest," they said. "Answer the kids' questions, but don't tell them more than they ask." I remembered this advice being similar to the advice we were given when our eldest son had asked about how babies were made. Somehow this situation now seemed much more complicated, but maybe that same answer works for most of life, a script of sorts. Never answer more than you are asked.

Our older sons, Henry and Theo, would understand my mom's death, our friends told us. The boys were thirteen and eleven, smart and mature. But Luke was only nine and didn't even want to talk about the fact that we had moved so far away from his grandparents and friends. Lucy was five and missed her grandma so much that every night before bed she looked at a photo book my mom had made for the grandchildren for Christmas just a few months before. After I read Lucy a picture book each night, she would sit in her twin bed and flip through the photo book of her life with her grandma. There were photos of Lucy and her brothers with their grandma, camping at Mormon Lake, riding roller coasters at Disneyland, reading books on the couch, hiking desert trails, zip-lining, and making chocolate chip cookies. My mom had created the twenty-four-page book that held more than one hundred photos, and personalized the book jacket, writing: "A gift from Grandma. Beautiful memories of wonderful times from the birth of all 4 of you, though you will be far away, our visits and phone calls will keep us together. This book is but a snapshot of Grandma, fun times with you of your life in Phoenix. I've loved every minute of having you so close and getting to share so many of your life experiences. You are very, very special to me and I am so proud of each of you. Send me pictures of your new home in Cincinnati and all of your fun activities. (No snowballs, though.) Love you, Grandma." Lucy kept the hardback photo book on the floor next to her bed.

When John and I came downstairs, the kids knew something was up, I could tell. They were quiet and waiting. None of us had our footing yet in our new city. The kids were trying to make friends, and John and I were trying to figure out our new jobs, the politics of the newsroom where we both worked, the quickest route to work, and where we could find good Mexican food. In Phoenix we always threw a huge party for Valentine's Day—the inaugural party was for families with four children because these couples were less likely to go out that night, and somehow with our four we seemed to attract families with four kids, too. Later, more families came, and in recent years the party had swelled to about eighty parents and children, flowing in and out of our ranch house in the warm February weather in Phoenix. Lucy cried that year when she realized we couldn't throw a party in Cincinnati—we had just moved a few weeks prior and didn't know enough people to invite.

"But we always have one," she argued, in a voice that was very much still five.

I had tried so hard to make everyone miss home a little less in those first few months—throwing a special party for Valentine's Day, just for the six of us. I decided to make it different so they would make a new memory, rather than miss what they didn't have. February fourteenth is Arizona's birthday and that year was the state's one hundredth birthday. I printed out place cards in the shape of the state to celebrate the centennial, something they had been studying in school back home before the move. I made carne asada tacos, guacamole, and a chocolate cake with white frosting and red sprinkles in the shape of a heart.

We sat around the table and talked about what we missed most and tried to get everyone to say what they liked best about their new home. Henry said he liked that he was going to learn to play lacrosse and would join the junior high team. Theo and Luke repeated what Henry said, seemingly deciding at that moment that lacrosse would be their sport, too.

When we got to Lucy, she crossed her arms.

"It's not home," she said in a defiant five-year-old voice. She already had been upset because she was the only one who had brought homemade valentines cards to students in her class at their party that day and felt embarrassed that everyone else had bought their valentines at the store and included candy.

"It *will* be home," Theo, who was eleven, told her, and scooted his chair closer to hers at the dining room table.

The kids had become even closer since the move, turning to each other because they didn't have anyone else. But Henry, at thirteen, had begun pushing away, and for the first time, he asked for his own room instead of sharing with his little brothers as he had since the younger boys had moved out of their cribs. So Theo, Luke, and Lucy shared a room, with Theo and Luke becoming best friends and letting Lucy tag along.

Now, John and I found the children waiting in the dining room, sitting on the wood floor, knees pulled up to their chests, lined up against the wall. We had been upstairs alone too long, and they must have heard me crying. My face was red and my eyes wet and swollen, which wasn't new, but part of who their mom had become of late. The move was hard on me, and coming to grips with the old secret of sex abuse, and its recent aftermath—telling my mom about it six months ago—had taken its toll on me. Then being so far away from her. And now she was gone.

There was no way around this, yet also no way to tell them the truth, so I remembered the words of my friends: Keep it simple.

I sat down on the floor next to my two youngest, crossed my legs, and took a deep breath.

"Grandma died," I said. "I'm so sorry."

Luke and Lucy crawled into my lap and both started crying. Henry looked afraid, afraid to move, to talk, to react or show emotion. Theo, eleven, wasted no time in asking me what had happened.

"Her heart stopped working," I said. It was true, it did stop working. Theo squinted his eyes at me in a way I could tell he questioned what I told him.

"But Grandma was healthy. She hiked every day and she was a heart nurse," he said. "She took care of people with bad hearts."

"Yes, she did," I said. "And she loved helping people get better after heart attacks."

"Well then why couldn't she stop her heart from stopping?"

"Theo," I said, "sometimes people are sick and it's hard to see." There was so much more truth to this statement than I realized.

We told Henry and Theo the truth later that night in private. I knew they both would want to hear more, that they both needed more, but they both knew not to ask in front of their little brother and sister.

I started to cry in a way that was so strong, so feral, so uncontrollable that I didn't even realize this might scare the children. The kids went upstairs to their rooms and I folded into the couch in the living room. John called my psychologist. Although she worked eleven miles away, she happened to be at a church four blocks from our house that night. She drove to our house and walked with me upstairs, sitting next to me on the side of the bed.

"It's my fault," I said, in a tone that was less crying and more just emotionless and dead.

"No," she said, and clasped her hands around mine.

The lasagna, I remembered. I yelled to John to take it out of the oven.

"Laura," she said. "Your mom made this choice. This is not your fault, not your doing."

The letter, I thought. I should not have sent the letter.

Three days before, I had written a letter to my mom. It was a letter I had started and stopped, written and deleted, and written again many times.

When I had told my mom about the abuse, six months before, in person, it had been difficult to talk to her about it, and it had become more difficult after the move. The distance made it hard to read each other; neither of us were able to say much, and I felt conversations ended with both of us feeling empty. My psychologist suggested that I write about what I had hidden for years, things I was trying to make myself and my mom see, to help my mom understand it, and to let her know we could survive it. The thought was that the letter would allow me to express how I felt to my mom, and my mom would have the words in front of her and could look to them again if she doubted my love for her. It would give my mom something to hold, to remind her of what was true, of how much I loved her, and to let her know that I wanted to make things right.

But now, I thought, it didn't matter why I wrote it, and now it didn't matter what I had said. My mom was gone and I felt responsible. I was certain I was responsible.

My psychologist kept reminding me that this was my mom's choice, my mom's decision, my mom's action, but it was so hard to believe. I tried to tell myself that my mom was gone because she wanted to be gone, but would I ever really know that?

Later, my sister and other people would share memories of my mom's life: the time my mom started a fire in the bathroom of our house. The year when we were little, and our grandma came to live with us because she was so worried about our mom. The time my mom bought a gun and told her best friend that she might use it on herself. The day my mom had said she wanted to walk in front of a truck. The days when my mom had been so depressed and tired from taking care of her husband who had been sick and continued to drink. But at that moment, I didn't know most of these pieces—they were fragmented memories that took place decades apart, never put together in one story by the people who loved her.

A few months before my mom died, in the fall of 2011, I sat in a Phoenix office with a psychologist, the first time I'd gone to see a counselor on my own. I had attended group counseling in college for an eating disorder, and even worked as a peer counselor in high school (the irony is not lost on me). But this time, I didn't know what was making me so sad, what was making me feel so lost and so not like myself. I didn't know how to fix it on my own. I felt broken, but I didn't understand why.

We explored work: I loved working at my hometown newspaper. We explored family: I had a great husband and our four amazing kids who were healthy and happy. I had close friends, but none whom I felt I could confide in. And I was empty lately, unable to feel much of anything. I was trying to figure out why I was so numb. I was trying to figure out what I needed to do to feel something.

This doesn't mean I was sad all the time. About a year before this moment, I had told my husband that I didn't know what was wrong with me, but something was wrong. I knew I should be happy; I knew I was lucky. But I couldn't feel it. I loved being a mom, but something tugged at me.

He had looked around at our life, which all looked wonderful. "It's almost Christmas," he said. "Things will get better." He had planned a surprise trip to Paris for my fortieth birthday the coming year. He said to trust him—things would get better.

So I listened, and went through the motions of life. And John was right, I could see that things were good: We had an amazing trip, the kids were great, work was interesting. But when we returned, something still felt missing, wrong; even things I liked doing felt hard; things that should make me happy weren't making me happy. I was afraid and I felt I was hurting people I loved. I didn't understand myself.

It didn't even cross my mind that maybe I was depressed. I thought depression looked like someone not able to get out of bed, someone who wasn't showering or going to work, someone who couldn't function. To me depression was someone who was sad all the time, someone who never laughed or had a good time. I couldn't see myself in that spot, and I couldn't see what was wrong. So that's why I was there, on that very firm couch, trying to find the right way to cross my legs to be comfortable while I was telling a stranger the worst things about me, the truths I hadn't revealed to anyone else, the very selfish feeling of having everything I should want, but feeling like part of me was missing. Was I ungrateful for this wonderful life I was lucky to have? I sat there feeling as if I were naked, which at that point felt like a better option than being in the counselor's office.

After talking through several sessions about my family and my life, my psychologist said she wanted to go further back. She asked about my childhood. It was good, I told her: We had dinner every night together, my mom sewed matching dresses for my big sister and me (I might have liked this much more than my sister did), we went to the library weekly and brought home as many books as we could carry, my dad coached my softball teams, my mom watched all our swim meets. We went to Mission Beach in San Diego every summer for vacation, we saw our cousins and family on every holiday and often in the days between. My mom had stayed at home when we were little—and I would find her watching soap operas and ironing when I got home from school. My mom started college when I was in fourth grade so that she could become a registered nurse. My mom juggled her classes and 1970s motherhood, which meant she led our Camp Fire Girl groups and went on school field trips and always made dinner. She taught me how to type so I could help her with her research papers. My dad worked for the state police as a forensic investigator. We were never rich, but we had what we needed, and we knew better than to ask for things we couldn't afford. We had Barbies and Legos, and my parents even saved for two years to buy me a piano when I decided I wanted to learn how to play. My mom sewed my prom dresses, my dad paid for a private pitching coach for softball.

It was good, I said. It was good, I said again, until slowly, the truth was revealed. The details came out one at a time, like from a leaky faucet, steady and slow at first, and then faster. The secret that had been stored in a part of my brain for decades needed to come out.

A few years after my parents divorced, my mom started dating a guy pretty seriously. He was patient and kind, never raising his voice. He had two children close in age to my sister and me, but they lived with their mother and her husband. My mom's boyfriend lived in a condominium a few miles away from our house; it smelled like tobacco from the pipe he smoked each night. He had two dachshunds and when they had puppies, we had taken the runt and named her Daisy. My mom's boyfriend drank a lot, and was frequently drunk, something my sister and I noticed shortly after meeting him.

I was fifteen when I first saw him naked.

That year, my mom sold the house I grew up in, and we moved into my mom's boyfriend's condominium. My sister was in college and lived in an apartment across the city. In this new place, my bedroom was on the second floor down the hallway from my mom and her boyfriend's bedroom. My new bedroom had a walk-in closet and a window that overlooked a narrow alley and a cinder-block wall. My mom had worked hard to make this new place feel like home—she wallpapered my new bedroom in the same 1980s mauve-and-teal paint-splattered wallpaper I had in my old bedroom, and hung the same Nagel prints that I had bought with Christmas money, and she found a new wicker desk to create a quiet place for me to study.

One night, a few months after moving in to the condo, I was in bed reading when my mom's boyfriend opened my bedroom door. I figured he needed to tell me something, but it was weird that he did not knock, or maybe he had simply opened the door to the wrong room. I thought he would likely say "excuse me" and leave, but instead, he walked in and closed the door behind him. It was weird, and I felt embarrassed. I sank lower under my covers, placing my paperback copy of *The Fountainhead* beside me, and wanted to reach up to turn out the light. My mom was already asleep—she got up at four each weekday morning to get to the hospital by five, and only stayed up past ten on Thursday nights when we watched *ER* together.

But my mom's boyfriend just stood there, staring straight at me. I thought maybe he was drunk—he was an alcoholic, always a giant plastic tumbler in his hand, Mountain Dew or RC Cola mixed with whiskey or vodka. He stood for a minute, and then began touching himself. I pretended I didn't see him, reasoning that if I didn't look up, he would realize he was in the wrong room and would walk out and we could all pretend it didn't happen. I was afraid to even reach up to turn off the light. I didn't move.

After thirty seconds or two minutes, I couldn't tell, he walked out of the room and closed the door behind him. I told myself that night that it had been a mistake, and I was more embarrassed for him than afraid. What kind of person gets so drunk they can't find their room in their own home? I figured he was so drunk that he wouldn't remember it, that he wouldn't even know it happened. In the morning I wondered if I had dreamed it. That couldn't have happened, right? It was too weird for me to understand, too weird to tell anyone—not my mom, my sister, or even my best friend. I reminded myself that he was a nice guy, that he adored my mom, and my mom adored him. I decided he'd simply had too much to drink—he frequently fell asleep in the family room on the couch, holding a glass of wine from a box, or a giant tumbler that he never seemed to spill. He must have turned the wrong way at the top of the stairs. We all could just pretend it never happened, because it seemed I was the only one who truly knew it happened.

I didn't have a lock on my bedroom door, so the next night I went to bed earlier, turning out the lights before my chemistry homework was finished. Part of me thought that the previous night was just a mistake, but what if it wasn't? I lay in my bed, my body stiff, shoulders up, jaw clenched, hands resting across my chest. I was afraid to move because I had a water bed and didn't want to make a noise, and I listened for any sound of him. He was usually pretty drunk at night, and I would hear not his footsteps on the carpeted stairs, but the sound of him stumbling into the walls on his way up. I figured that if coming in to my room was a mistake, it wouldn't happen again, but if it did, I didn't want to have to see it.

I heard him reach the top of the stairs. Turn right, turn right, go to bed, I whispered to myself. Just go right. Don't come in, don't come in, don't come in, I repeated, closing my eyes. Don't come in.

I heard my door open.

My bed sat about seven feet to the right of the door; a small table with a skirt stood next to it, one of those heavy French Victorian reproduction–style phones that had been my eighth-grade graduation present on top of it. I thought maybe he would trip as he walked closer, jarring him to reality and from whatever he was doing. The room wasn't completely dark—light still snuck in through the edges of the miniblinds, illuminating enough that when I opened my eyes, I could see him.

He walked up to the edge of the bed—this time he wore a pair of short running shorts and didn't wear a T-shirt. He looked straight at me and told me not to say anything. I didn't know what he wanted. I was fifteen. What did he mean, not to say anything to him? I felt confused and frightened and all I wanted was for this not to be happening.

"Don't tell anyone," he said, as he kissed me. He smelled like citrus and vodka and pipe smoke, and the bed whooshed as he moved on top of me. I both wanted the sound to wake up my mom so she would rush in and was equally terrified that she would. What was he doing? Why was he doing this? I kept trying to figure out if it was really happening, yet I was afraid to make a sound.

I told him that night that I was a virgin, thinking maybe he would stop as his hands reached under my T-shirt and down into my underpants. He told me he knew that wasn't true, that I had a boyfriend and my mom had put me on birth control pills. He told me to stop lying to him.

I was quiet, feeling his weight, and his hands moving to places I didn't want them. I was afraid and thought about grabbing that heavy phone by the bed and hitting him on the head, but I worried that then I would have to explain to my mom what had happened. I simply froze. I kept thinking about her and how she was happy for what seemed to be the first time in a long time. She'd been so unhappy after the divorce, so unsure of herself. She had her confidence now, joy, and I couldn't ruin that, I told myself, no matter what he did to me. Close your eyes, count backward from ten, and again, until it is over.

He pushed inside me. I tried not to make a sound. Ten, nine, eight, seven . . . over and over.

Before he left the room, he reminded me not to say anything: "Your mom will never believe you. No one will believe you."

Instead of wondering why he did this, I questioned myself on why I let it happen, why I didn't try to push him away, why I didn't scream or yell at him, why I didn't try to get away and run to tell my mom. It was 1986, and even though priests had been abusing children for decades, it would be another decade at least until the abuse would be reported and become public. It was way before the #MeToo movement, when we still qualified things as "date rape" and I didn't know anyone who had ever even talked about sex abuse, let alone told their story. It wasn't in any of the after-school specials I had watched, nor did we talk about it in health class. I don't think I even had words to bring it up, so I didn't. Would anyone think it was my fault? Would I be to blame?

Push it to a corner of your brain and leave it there. Don't think about it. Between the ages of fifteen and nineteen, I would see his figure in my door, my mom asleep down the hall. He would come into my room, always smelling of whiskey or vodka and pipe smoke. On weekends, I would sleep over at my best friend's house to avoid him. I never invited her to stay at my house, always making excuses for why we should sleep over at her house.

For years, my stepfather raped me. I never screamed, I never kicked him, never tried to hit him or bite him; I pushed back, but quietly. I weighed one hundred pounds and he was twice my size. "Stay quiet," he told me, "and your mom won't be mad at you." He knew how close I was with my mom, but he also knew how happy she was. He knew how much I loved her, and that I would never do anything to ruin her happiness. I also knew that letting him do this meant I could never get in trouble at home, no matter what I did. He wouldn't tell if I stayed out past my curfew, wouldn't tell if I hadn't taken out the garbage or not done my chores. It was confusing to me because he was so nice to my mom and to me at other times. He was so easygoing and so easy to get along with—people always liked him. He doted on my mom, and although he didn't see his children that often, he seemed to adore them, too. He was a racist and talked terribly about Mexicans even though my father was Mexican American, and I hated his conservative politics that meant Rush Limbaugh was a frequent family-room guest on the radio, but he was nice to my mom. And my mom seemed at ease, happy. So I learned to use it to my advantage in lithe ways, if that makes sense. I figured if my mom was happy, I could be happy. Yet like many victims of sexual abuse, I took out the pain on myself.

I stopped eating during my senior year of high school, dropping to ninety and then eighty-five pounds. I worked hard to be nearly perfect in school. My high school yearbook shows me in photos for the Academic Decathlon team, the Honor Society, the school newspaper as its editor, student government, the softball team, Girls State, the culture club, and pretty much any other club that gave me a valid reason to leave the house. When the urge to tell my mom felt strong, I cut lines on the outside of my thighs with a Swiss Army knife I received in my Christmas stocking. I wanted to feel something, to create pain and remind myself how bad she would feel. I could help make us both happy.

I was relieved when I started my freshman year of college at a school in Northern California, escaping life at home for a while. When I moved into my dorm, my roommate had already built our beds into a loft style, sitting just two feet from the ceiling. Even though I hated the idea of climbing a ladder every night and sleeping up so high, the truth was, it felt so much more comfortable and safe than at home.

At Christmas break that freshman year, a new friend drove with me back to Arizona. She wanted to spend a week in the warm Phoenix winter before returning to the snowy Midwest. I was grateful to have made a friend at a school where I hadn't known anyone—and that I could show her my hometown. But I was afraid, too. Where would she sleep? Would my mom's husband try to rape her, too?

She and I stayed out late each night of our break, and I thought maybe if we didn't come home until he was asleep we would be fine. But when we got home, he often was still up, sitting on the couch watching TV with the volume way too loud. My friend slept in my bed, and I slept on the floor in a sleeping bag in front of her. He avoided my room that week until she went home, and then the familiar and sick routine returned.

I found safety when I returned to my college and dorm room that January, throwing myself into school, my work-study job, and writing for the university's newspaper and radio station. I grew nervous when spring break neared and I would have to return home.

After five years of dating or living together, my mom and her boyfriend were married that summer after my freshman year of college in 1989. They held a small ceremony at my aunt's cabin in the mountains of northern Arizona, about ninety minutes south of the Grand Canyon. My mom wore a peach sundress I bought her with my discount working at The Limited that summer. My sister and I held hands as we watched them recite vows while a very hippie-like spiritual woman from Flagstaff married them. I thought maybe this would be it—they were married and maybe things would change. I felt hopeful for the first time, but when they got back from their honeymoon with friends on a sailboat in the Bahamas, the abuse resumed.

The summer between my sophomore and junior years of college, I became an exchange student in Poland and then traveled through Europe instead of looking for a journalism internship in Phoenix so I could avoid living at home.

Two years later, I graduated from college and moved home for a few months before my job at a newspaper in New Mexico was to start. My mom's husband offered me a job in his bicycle shop, doing inventory and converting his store from analog to digital. I was wary, but needed the money. He never touched me again. We worked alongside each other in the bike store many days as if it never happened. We talked politics—or argued about politics—

discussed what he could surprise my mom with for her birthday, about getting another dog, about everything but what had happened. Neither of us ever said a word about it, not to each other or anyone else. I blocked it from my mind for decades, telling no one.

A few years after graduating from college, I met John in Albuquerque. We both lived there for work, neither of us connected to this city that was great for news, and cheap for two young journalists, but we wanted something more. We moved to Portland, Oregon, got married, and a few years later had our first son, Henry. We moved to my hometown of Phoenix, a bigger market and a better job for John who worked as a TV news producer, and the real reason—I could be closer to my mom again. I hated that in Henry's first year, my mom had seen him only three times. Now she lived just a few miles away and we had Sunday dinner at my mom and her husband's home, camped with them in their motor home in northern Arizona, and took care of their yellow Labrador retriever, Bailey, and then later, their next yellow Lab, Moe. I had three more children and life moved along as it does. I pretended the abuse never happened, until one day, I couldn't.

After a few appointments with my psychologist that fall of 2011, I told about what I had kept inside for decades. I told her about the abuse as if it were a confession, as if it had been my fault, for all these years. I had lived a lie by not telling my mom or husband or anyone about this, and now I felt relief, like something I had ignored and kept inside for so long finally could be told. Maybe I felt safe now. My mom's husband had been sick after a stroke and a brain tumor, and he still was drinking, a lot. After his stroke, he had to live in a rehabilitation facility for a while before he was well enough to come home. It felt as if he no longer was a threat, even if maybe he hadn't been for years.

My mom asked me to bring their dog to visit him one day at the rehab center while she was at work. I knew how stressed she had been, and how busy, and I wanted to be helpful. I didn't want to go, but did anyway for her. I had seen him so many times over the years, but I hadn't been alone with him since I was maybe twenty-one. One of the assistants at the rehab center brought his wheelchair out to the grassy courtyard; he was strapped at the waist and chest so he wouldn't fall out. His arms rested weak at his sides. I walked Moe up to him on her leash.

My mom's husband looked at me that day and said, "You're real pretty, like your mom."

I took a step back.

"Come give me a kiss," he said, his words slurring.

This time, I didn't have to, and I'm not sure I had to before, but I had thought I had no choice. People have said that before you die, your life flashes before your eyes. I don't know if that's true, but I do know that in a blink that day I saw everything he had done to me. It was as if I was watching a reel of life with him: I saw myself trying to be still on a super-single water bed, my eyes fixed on the paint-splattered wallpaper. I smelled the Jack Daniel's that still makes my stomach turn. I heard him say that my mom would never believe me. I saw him in my doorway and felt the resignation of knowing it was time. I saw myself lying on my back pretending to be somewhere else while he pushed inside. I remembered the fear and the determined feeling that I could make it through. I saw my mom becoming so happy—when she learned to water-ski and sail a catamaran with him. I saw her coming home with her first wet suit after learning to scuba dive with him. I saw her smile—not a forced smile, just a relaxed smile. I remembered not wanting to ruin it. I remembered counting backward.

It's "really pretty," I thought—he should say "really pretty," not "real pretty." The adjective in this sentence should be *really,* not *real*. My mind had gone to the familiar, the routine that would calm my brain—not numbers, but grammar rules.

But I wasn't a teenager this time. I was a mom and I wasn't afraid. I pulled on the dog's leash, turned around, and walked to the car, leaving him in the courtyard alone.

The feeling was both startling and scary, knowing that he had the ability to bring all of this back with one small phrase. My psychologist said I had pushed the memory of the sex abuse so far back that I never dealt with what happened to me other than at the emotional level. When other things in my life weren't going right—when my mom's husband said he wanted a kiss, for example—it triggered that memory and brought it forward. The fact that I had turned forty and finally felt strong in my life provided a time to tell. She said that holding little traumas inside your head can allow them to attach to each other, creating one big trauma that no longer wants to be contained. At a certain point, you no longer can compartmentalize them. People act out, she said, sometimes in harmful ways: drinking, drugs, reckless sex, eating disorders, cutting, shoplifting. The mind finds ways to placate itself, as mine had over the years.

After a few more appointments, my psychologist suggested I needed to tell my mom about the abuse. First I told

John. He agreed that I needed to tell my mom. It was a lie between my mom and me, one that would keep us from being close, no matter how close I thought we were. I was so afraid that telling my mom would upset her, that it would make her feel bad, that it would be something that once I shared, I wouldn't be able to hide back in my head. I knew my mom's husband was sick, and that he had been such an alcoholic that maybe she would understand and maybe she would look back and see that there were signs she missed. Maybe she would remember how drunk he was, maybe she had seen this behavior other places.

In the years he was in our lives, did my mom notice that I never wanted to be around him alone, that after I was married he was only invited to our house with her on holidays or on special occasions, that she always came over alone? Did my mom understand when I told her that the kids should never be alone with him? Did she think it was only because of his drinking problem? Why didn't she ask why? I didn't think about how maybe she was stretched thin taking care of him, that his drinking and his care had weakened her, that she hadn't been sleeping well, and that maybe she only knew the good in him, that maybe this would be too much for her.

My mom stopped by my house one evening that fall. She had retired from work and spent most of her time caring for her husband. She still came over to see the kids, but didn't stay for dinner as often or read to them before bed because she wanted to get home to her husband—she didn't want to leave him alone for long. That night, she parked her Jeep in front of our house. I was outside watching the kids play soccer in the yard, the grass starting to brown as the cooler

Phoenix temperatures set in. As usual, the kids ran up to my mom to hug her, calling out "Grandma, Grandma," to tell her about something from the day. Lucy tugged on my mom's cardigan to come inside and read her a book. I was quiet. We stayed outside to enjoy a night finally cool enough for the mosquitoes to be gone, but still warm enough for the kids to wear shorts.

John came home soon and brought the kids inside. I had only recently told him about the abuse and he knew I wanted to talk to my mom. He was upset with her, thinking she didn't protect me, that she should have seen something, seen the abuse, should have recognized what was happening. It was easier for him to be mad at her than for me to be. He hadn't known her back then, hadn't known our life, and only saw what was happening now. It hurt him that I had kept this from him and that now I was falling apart and hurting our family.

I told my mom that I had something difficult to tell her, but that I needed to do it. She looked worried.

"Are you OK?" she asked.

"I am," I said. "But I'm worried about you."

I told her that her husband had raped me when I was a teenager, shortly after we moved in with him during high school.

She didn't say she didn't believe me, and she didn't seem surprised. She didn't reach over to hug me, didn't ask how, didn't say she was sorry. She didn't cry, didn't seem angry, had almost no reaction. She left without saying goodbye to the kids, and went home to him.

I struggled to understand her response, or her lack of response, to this betrayal of her daughter, her family, her trust.

But I didn't understand. Had she known that this happened? I couldn't imagine that she could have known and didn't stop it. But I couldn't understand how she could seem so calm after hearing this, how she didn't look troubled. I didn't think about how maybe she was depressed and couldn't react.

I walked inside the house, pretended everything was fine, and sat down to read Lucy a Henry and Mudge book, a gift from my mom, who had left notes in cursive handwriting on the pages about the characters and pictures. I tried to concentrate on the words, on Lucy's hands holding the book and turning the pages, instead of how my mom hadn't seemed angry, didn't seem to feel anything. I was so angry and so sad. I had thought I might feel better somehow letting her know what happened, but instead I felt worse.

I now think neither of us knew how to react. I think both of us were depressed and neither of us were expressing exactly how we felt, and maybe we were feeling so much, we didn't *know* how we felt. But I couldn't see any of this then—I was stuck in simply feeling hurt, and confused.

I read the book to Lucy again. I knew how to handle things that were difficult by putting them in a part of my brain, compartmentalizing. Instead of counting backward this time, I read the book over and over as many times as Lucy asked that night. She climbed into my lap and I held the book as she then read parts of it to me.

That fall and through winter, my mom and I didn't talk about the abuse. In many ways, we pretended we had never had the conversation. I said nothing to her about it, but everything hurt inside. She said nothing about it to me. We talked, but not about that; we talked about the kids, about my work, about her dog, about the birds that show up in the morning outside her window, about her fall garden that bloomed. John grew angry with my mom for letting this happen and how it was exploding now and ruining what felt like our perfect family. I was clearly depressed, but didn't realize it at the time.

John had long wanted to move back to the Midwest, closer to Chicago where he grew up, and where his parents lived. We had spent the past nineteen years in the West, living in New Mexico where we met, Oregon, and then the past fourteen years in Phoenix raising our family. I was ready to move up in the editing chain in my company, so it seemed time for a change. Maybe we just needed a break, and maybe moving to a new place would help—I could leave all this in Phoenix.

We had started looking at jobs in other places when an editor role opened in Cincinnati. The company that owned our newspaper in Phoenix also owned a newspaper in Cincinnati, a half-day's drive to John's parents' house. I hoped the company might transfer John and me. I didn't tell my mom when we flew to Ohio to interview and then to house hunt. It hurt to not talk to her about one of the most important decisions in my life at the time. It hurt to not be able to talk through it with her, to tell her about the cute brick houses that seemed to be everywhere in the Midwest, about the school that the kids could walk to, about how it snowed enough to make the city look dusted in powdered sugar as we explored neighborhoods. It hurt to think I might no longer see her any day I wanted. It hurt to think of driving home from work and not seeing her Jeep in front of my house and knowing that everything inside would be fine. It hurt thinking the kids wouldn't be able to see her every week, that they wouldn't know her in the same way. And that she would lose that closeness with them. It hurt thinking that I wouldn't be able to just call her on my drive to work, like I had done every day since I got a cellphone. Everything about our relationship hurt and I felt as if it was my fault.

In the next few weeks, she stopped by in the afternoon to see the kids. Some days she would still be there when I came home from work. We talked, but it was mostly facts, no feelings. Something big sat between us, and neither of us knew how to move through. The fact that I hadn't told her long ago created a secret. I didn't want to make her feel bad and didn't want her to think I was angry at her, because to me I wasn't angry—I blamed myself for telling her now. I felt I was selfish to not tell her then when the abuse happened, and selfish to tell her now because I thought I needed to. I wanted to take it all back and hold it again. I had lived with it for that long—why couldn't I have continued? So we ignored what I had said and the abuse, for two months.

Slowly, her denial and her lack of reaction began to give way, and she started asking me questions. She wanted to know how she hadn't sensed anything, how the man she knew, the one with a gentle heart who once hired a homeless man to work in his bike shop, who used his van to help people move, who kept our beloved dachshund Daisy until the dog was well into her twenties, could do this. He had taught my mom to ski and sail and scuba dive and to become much more adventurous. How could he be capable of this? And even more, how could she not have suspected it? She was so confused that I had let them both back into my life now after what he did that it made her brain unable to even think this could be possible. She tried to reconcile that these two men were the same person.

I told her I felt like I had to tell her, that part of the secret was in keeping it. If I was never alone with him again, I could pretend it never happened. My mom and I went days without talking, then talked until we both couldn't breathe from crying.

My mom came over the day before we were set to move from Phoenix to Cincinnati in late January of 2012. She helped me pack the last boxes, and we shared sushi, our favorite lunch choice. Neither of our husbands or my kids liked sushi, so it had become our treat. We stood in the kitchen, eating at the counter, and talked mostly about the kids. She was going to miss them so much and I knew how much they would miss her, so much so, I could barely mention it. She talked about how much they were going to like the snow, and we recounted all the gloves, hats, and coats I had bought for the kids in the past few weeks. We packed the last box with the final things my mom said to put in there—paper towels, plates, cups, bleach wipes, toilet paper, a packet of instant mashed potatoes she insisted I would be happy to find—things she said would be good to open first when we arrived at our new house. I hugged my mom standing in the kitchen that day and I felt as if I were hugging a black hole, like she wasn't even there. If a hug could feel empty, this was it.

The alarm was set for five in the morning to load four kids and a dog in a minivan and drive eighteen hundred miles across the country. I held on to her and tried not to cry. Her shoulders felt narrow. I could feel her ribs in the back.

"I love you, Mom," I said. "Always."

"Love you, kiddo," she said.

She suggested that she come by in the morning to say goodbye before we left, but we were leaving so early—hours before the sun was up—so the children could sleep the first few hours of the trip. I told her that it might be easier if she didn't come.

On the four-day drive across the country, I took photos and posted them on Instagram as a way to document the trip for my mom. I had taught her how to use Instagram, and my mom was still so new to it that she didn't have a profile photo yet, just the gray silhouette. We both hadn't posted much of anything on it, so it felt like our own diary, in a way, more private than Facebook as we each only had a few followers. I experimented with filters and posted photos of the kids sleeping, or Lucy with her hair blowing in the wind with the window open, of the dog somehow asleep, yet sitting up. My mom wrote silly comments on my photos about us seeing snow for the first time on the road trip, and happy comments about places we stopped, always ending with "Love you," "Love you all."

Chapter 2

A Growing Distance

MOST DAYS DURING the first month we lived in Cincinnati, I called my mom on my drive to work. She wasn't sleeping well, and seemed to be almost always awake. I took a route that snaked along the Ohio River, and would tell her what I saw as I drove. She missed the change of seasons, having moved to Arizona from Nebraska as a teenager. I told her about the barges on the Ohio—it was an actual working river. I still can't drive that road without hearing her voice, and mostly I drive a different route to work to avoid it.

One morning, as I told her how beautiful it was when you could start seeing the downtown buildings on the drive in, the crown on the Great American Tower, the row houses in Mt. Adams that remind me of San Francisco, the curve of the Reds baseball stadium, she told me she'd been to Cincinnati once, as a young girl. She hadn't told me before that she had ever visited, and I wanted to know more. She said she didn't remember much, but they visited a big department store downtown and she got to shop for her Christmas dress. Was it still there? she asked, trying to remember the name.

"Maybe Shillito's," I said.

"Yes," she said, excited that I knew the name. "It had fancy windows decorated with elves at Christmastime."

I told her the department store wasn't here anymore, but the name is so well known I had heard of it after only living here a month. Part of the building now holds apartments, I told her, and downtown is so pretty, there was a big Christmas tree in the center of downtown with an ice rink. And soon, I told her, the crocuses and tulips would sprout up in spring. Our three youngest kids walk through a gorgeous little wooded area to get to school. I said that one day, she would get to visit and walk with them through the little forest, that she would see Theo and Luke play baseball, and see how Lucy could now do the monkey bars. We had a guest room for her with its own bathroom. Three of the kids shared a room, so even with a four-bedroom house, we had a room just for her. I also told her that Lucy wanted a sleepover with her grandma and wanted her to sleep in the trundle bed in the room she shared with Theo and Luke. Lucy told me to tell my mom that if she wanted, my mom could sleep in the top bed and Lucy below in the trundle. They could look at the "Grandma book" together and tell stories.

My mom said she couldn't leave her husband by himself for very long. Sometime, she said, she would come visit. I thought back to when I first had told her we were moving to Ohio—she had found a good price on a plane ticket to Cincinnati and wanted to make a reservation. I told her to wait until we actually moved, that I didn't know what my work schedule would be, what the kids would be doing, what might be best for us. I had told her to wait. I didn't think about what was best for her, that maybe she needed something to look forward to, a break of sorts.

A month before she died, I was having a terrible night. I had come from therapy where we once again reviewed that the sex abuse was not my fault and that I needed to stop feeling so guilty about it. I called my mom, trying to understand how her husband could have done this to me. I was angry— angry that it happened, angry at him, at myself for not telling her, not telling John, not telling anyone, and I directed my anger at her, in the way perhaps that sometimes only a daughter can do. It was a display of anger that felt like a tantrum, of emotions bottled up for thirty years free-flowing without a cap, without a way to stop them or even slow them. While she and I talked or mostly cried on the phone about how sorry she was, and about how much it hurt me, and how sorry I was and how much I missed her and needed her, she confronted him. I never had. And I don't know if she had. I could hear her yelling at her husband, while she held the phone: "Did you do this? Did you?"

He kept saying, "I don't remember. I don't remember."

She was so angry, yelling at him again and again: "Why did you do this?" I was silent, listening to their conversation from the spot where I sat on the kitchen floor. The call ended with nothing resolved, only sadness and anger and both of us in tears, and his saying he didn't remember.

Her husband was sixty-six and sick. He still drank too much, and a brain tumor and a stroke had left him dependent on her. My mom and I had been circling each other warily, each apologizing to the other. Nothing seemed resolved. I wrote and deleted and rewrote a letter, finally hitting Send.

Nothing I wrote told her anything that she didn't already know or that I hadn't told her, but the letter spelled out that her husband had abused me for years, how hard it was to have him come into my room so many nights, and then there was this: I didn't tell her then because I had wanted her to be happy. I told her I didn't forgive her, because I didn't need to forgive her. It wasn't her fault. It was his.

I told her I loved her and needed her. I wanted her to know the truth of what happened, the reason I didn't tell her, and that eventually we would be fine. But now I believe I saw only what I needed to see, neglecting to understand what she needed or what she was going through.

I never talked to her after I sent this letter. I thought the letter would make it all OK, that it would make her feel better. I wanted her to not just hear it, but to see it in print— that I didn't blame her, and that I loved her.

We're not supposed to blame ourselves when someone we love kills themselves, but many of us do anyway. After my mom died, the letter gnawed at me. Also, what if I had let her buy that plane ticket to visit? What if I hadn't moved away? What if I'd kept quiet about my stepfather? What if I'd never sent that letter? What if I had answered her phone call the morning she died? The "what if" questions held me in the tightest grip at night, keeping me awake counting backward until the sun peeked through the shades. All of them tried to answer: Was I to blame?

I reviewed what my mom's life had been like before she died, or at least the part I could see. So much of it seemed great, or better than great. She was a retired nurse and hospital administrator who had saved her money responsibly and had a solid pension. She was adored by my children and my sister's four children. She was in a book club and had close friends she hiked with weekly in the desert paths just outside her front door. While she hated that four of her grandchildren had moved so far away, my sister's children lived close, and she had planned to visit us soon. I know her husband had been sick, but he'd been sick for a while. He had been in a rehabilitation center after his stroke. Doctors recommended he go into a nursing home, but she wanted to bring him home. She devoted her life to taking care of him, getting him to therapy appointments, making sure he was exercising, and he had been improving. My mom's mom was still alive and healthy and lived in town with my mom's sister. My mom took trips with her friends to a cabin to fish and hike; she went to church and wrote letters to my kids. She strung beads together into jewelry and volunteered at a homeless shelter. She had traveled the world. She bought a house set into the side of a mountain, nestled among elm and ash trees that sometimes made you feel as if you were in a tree house.

I needed to find out what about her I had missed. I needed to know, to understand how someone who seemed to have so much, and who seemed so happy, could in fact be so sad. Or could you be both, and sometimes one of them won?

I combed through my mom's life, looking for clues. I learned she had been seeing a psychologist and psychiatrist and had been prescribed antidepressants. I better saw the strain that her husband's illness and his alcoholism were taking on her. She had started to attend weekly meetings for partners of alcoholics to learn to cope. I talked to my sister and my dad's sisters, tried to ask questions of my grandma and aunt, but they had little or nothing to say. Later I drove 966 miles to Florida to spend a week with my mom's best friend from when I was a child to find out if my mom had been depressed when I was young.

I learned everything I could from doctors who study suicide notes, from psychiatrists who personalize medicine to treat depression. I would learn that suicide had become the tenth leading cause of death in the United States in 2018, with numbers increasing in almost every state, and that money for research to better understand it remained low.[1] I explored the ripples of sexual abuse. I struggled not to follow her as I walked closer to this edge myself.

But first, we needed to say goodbye.

The day before my mom's funeral, the church where her service was to be held was quiet. It was May and already one hundred degrees in Phoenix. I walked past the meditation chapel at the Franciscan Renewal Center, past the white stucco buildings with red tile roofs that looked like they could be found at a resort in Santa Barbara, through a healing garden and rock labyrinth, and under the shade of palo verde trees to stop by the main office. The church, also known as the Casa, is run by the Order of the Friars Minor, part of the Franciscan family, and is owned by the Franciscan Friars Province of Saint Barbara, which works in cooperation with the Catholic diocese. This was an important distinction for my mom, and the reason I was there that day.

When my parents divorced, the priest at our neighborhood parish where I had been baptized and celebrated my First Communion told my mom that as a divorced woman whose marriage wasn't annulled, she was no longer welcome. It wasn't that she simply was no longer welcome to take Communion, but that she really shouldn't come back. We would later learn that at that same time, priests within the diocese were moved from one parish to the next for abusing children. My mom was devastated that her church had turned its back on her, especially when she felt as if she needed it more than ever. She discovered the Casa, a welcoming Catholic church that accepted her without question.

I needed to find the priest, the one my sister said our mom had talked to after Sunday Mass, just four days before she died. I asked for him by name at the front office and the church secretary came back with a man with a trim white beard and round wire-rimmed glasses. I followed him into a counseling room where the whir of the ceiling fan competed with his gentle voice. I wanted to know what he remembered about my mom. Tell me, I asked, what she was like when you last saw her. Did she seem sad? Was she depressed? I wanted to know.

He said he couldn't tell me what he had discussed with my mom because he didn't want to disclose confidential pastoral conversations with me. But on the last day he saw her, he said, she told him she thought she was fine, better even. He knew that she had been seeing a psychiatrist and was receiving counseling from him. She told him she thought she didn't need any more counseling. He said he was surprised and that he shook his head when my mom told him this.

"I told her I didn't think she was ready to stop coming yet," he said.

I have learned that when some people decide to kill themselves, they seem more at ease than they have in a long time, because they know that if they show any suicidal signs or too much distress, others might try to talk them out of it. It is an irrational idea, of course. I wondered if my mom thought she actually was getting better that Sunday, or if she was thinking her pain would end soon with her suicide so she wanted to let her priest know she was fine. Or did she really think she was OK that day? The rational mind doesn't kill itself. The body wants to live—even a dying body tries to preserve function to live.

I hadn't been to church in years. I was raised Catholic, received my Holy First Communion, but never was confirmed. In junior high school, I was waiting in line for confession that I needed to make to be confirmed. I decided that if my mom wasn't welcome in the church, I wasn't joining—not wanting to be part of a church that didn't include her. (I also didn't want to tell the priest I had borrowed my sister's new Esprit dress without asking or that I had skipped PE that week to watch a soap opera at my friend's house, so perhaps my skipping confession wasn't completely altruistic.) I went to a Jesuit university and took the required religion classes. John and I got married at St. Agnes Catholic Church in a ceremony so Catholic that we brought roses to the statue of the Virgin Mary. We baptized all four of our children in the Catholic church where my father-in-law was a deacon, in part to please my in-laws and in part so that our children could wear a baptismal gown passed down for four generations in my husband's family.

But my faith had faltered over the years, and we never pursued a First Communion for any of our children. I struggled with the very notion of faith. I understood and believed in the concept of church as a spiritual home for many, a community of people who care. We tried an Episcopal

church for a while when our kids were little, liking the familiar rituals and liturgy but also the liberal views allowing gay
marriage and women to be ordained as ministers. But we
hadn't been to church since we moved to Ohio. I still didn't
know if I believed in God, but I knew my mom did, and I
knew her faith had been important to her. And so that is
why I was there.

I asked the priest if my mom was OK. I thought he could
explain where she was now, tell me about redemption and
heaven. I wanted him to tell me she was now safe and at
peace. I wanted a fable, I think, of clouds and white robes,
of angels and comfort.

He nodded and reminded me that he couldn't tell me anything, that what she had told him was in confidence.

"But what else?" I asked him.

"All families are difficult," he said. "Some families just
know it, and others don't."

I sat down in one of the reclining chairs, frustrated.

"I just need to know if she is OK. I need to know that
she's in heaven."

I wanted a simple answer that only a believer could give
me, speaking about another believer. The whole purpose of
believing, I thought at the time, was to know people would
be saved when they died, that devotion to Jesus and the
prayers and readings meant they had somewhere to go when
they died, that they would be taken care of, redeemed.

Instead of answering, the priest sat down on the sofa
across from me and told me a story about his own mom who
had died, and how on an autumn day a few years ago when
he was lying in a hammock here at the church, he saw her
again. He was in the shade of the trees on one of those mag-

ical fall days, the kind after the summer heat breaks, a day that reminds you why you live in the desert. His mom came to him and they talked, or maybe, he said, he was just napping and it was all a dream. "Either way, I felt her presence," he told me. "So we don't know what is in the beyond."

"That's it?" I said, standing up. "You have nothing else?"

He nodded. "We can't know what is beyond this earthly life. We can only know our faith."

I wanted to talk to another priest who might tell me my mom was at peace, or that she was in heaven, or someone who understood that I needed to hear it.

My sister and I had agreed on a few things: I would write our mom's obituary, our mom would be cremated, the service would be at the Franciscan Renewal Center. We called her service a celebration of life, as if there was such a thing in the moment. We wanted to create a service we thought she would want at the church where she attended mass on Saturday evenings or Sunday mornings. My sister, who had been close with my aunt and grandma since she was little, had planned the service with them and the staff at the Casa before I arrived back in Phoenix.

One of my mom's favorite places was her garden. In the house where I grew up, she planted irises and sweet peas, roses and marigolds, flowers that stood up to the summer heat. When we moved into her boyfriend's tiny condo, my mom planted a rosebush in the little fenced courtyard outside our front door to start a new garden. My mom had sold our childhood home back to my dad that year, and one night I had mentioned to her that my dad was out of town, and she said, "Let's go." She took a shovel and drove to our old house where she dug up the plants and their bulbs and took them back to our new home, replanting them in the court-yard.

I remembered this story when my sister and I thought about what sort of flowers we wanted at her funeral. Would irises be the most appropriate? But we also knew my mom loved flowers straight from her garden—she loved when flowers looked less orderly, and more wild. So we asked that friends bring flowers to the funeral from their own yards or someone else's yard. As the church began to fill for the funeral, roses and mums, prickly red lantana and yellow branches of the palo verde lined the church in vases my sister had collected from her house and our mom's house.

My boys had dress shirts, but no jackets, and Theo wore his gray lace-up Vans, something my mom would have liked; we hadn't had time to buy new dress clothes. Lucy wore a new watercolor floral dress, a leftover Easter dress that had been on the clearance rack at Target. She held tight to Fred, a stuffed dog that was recently handed down to her by her biggest brother, Henry. He had carried it since he was three. Theo was only seventeen months older than Luke and the two were about the same height, but Luke reached out for his older brother's hand.

The prayer cards for my mom had St. Francis, patron saint of animals, on them, of course, for all the times my mom brought her dog, Moe, with her to mass for the annual blessing of the animals. The card read, "And the God of all grace, who called you to his eternal glory in Christ, after you have suffered a little while, will himself restore you and make you strong, firm and steadfast" (1 Pet. 5:10). I tried to persuade myself to believe that after all this suffering, God somehow now would take care of my mom, that she would indeed be strong again. Or at least she likely believed this, and that is what mattered, not what I thought. Maybe the priest hadn't exactly said this, but the Bible verse did.

I stopped in the bathroom to grab tissues before the service and saw my aunt, the one whose cabin we stayed at every summer in northern Arizona while growing up, the place we learned to fish and cross-country ski, where we skipped rocks and built a secret fort overlooking Mormon Lake, the place my mom and stepfather got married. My aunt resembles my mom with her blue eyes and her thin long arms. She seemed to be the best substitute for my mom, and I reached in for a hug. She put her stiff arms on my shoulders and told me to make sure my children didn't say hello to her mom, my children's great-grandma. "Stay away," she said. "Just stay away."

I was confused, and started to cry, not understanding what she meant by it. I reminded myself of something my psychologist had said: Everyone grieves differently and we must all give others grace. I just wanted to get a tissue and return to my family who was waiting in the lobby of the chapel. We walked up the center aisle to my grandma, who sat in a pew in the front row in the middle of the church, directly in front of the altar. I wanted to ask my grandma what happened to my mom, what she knew, the parts of my mom's story she understood, her truth—not right then, but one day. Right then, I just needed a hug and somehow thought my grandma's hug could fill in for my mom. I reached in, and my grandma looked at me, my husband, and our four children, and waved us off.

I didn't understand, but my grandma had lost her youngest girl, my mom, her Lucy. Maybe everyone was so sad that they couldn't deal with anyone else's emotions? Was it just too much to process on their own?

I learned later that my grandma blamed me, as did my mom's sister and her brother. My mom had told them that I had told her about the abuse by her husband. They saw how upset she was, how fragile she was, how much she struggled with this news. Instead of being angry on my behalf at my mom's husband, they were mad at me. I should have carried that with me, they believed. I was selfish to tell my mom and I had only told her to make myself feel better, they said. To free myself. They thought I shouldn't have told my mom when they thought she wasn't strong enough to hear it. They knew more than I did at this time, how my mom was doing, how much she was struggling, things I didn't know. Guilt wrapped its way around the grief.

We took a pew behind my sister and her family on the right side of the church facing the altar. My grandma and my mom's brother and sister sat in the pews in the front row in the middle of the church, which filled with neighbors I hadn't seen since I was a child: patients my mom helped recover from heart attacks in her work at the hospital, friends and former co-workers from the newspaper in Phoenix where I had worked, my dad and his family, and so many people I had never seen—more evidence that you never fully live in the world your parents do, especially when you are grown-up.

The service was about to start and I hadn't seen my mom's husband. I was both afraid to see him and also worried that he wasn't there. Was he sick? Did he not have a ride? Should we have made sure he had a ride there? I turned around and scanned the church, looking for him. Part of me thought that after the service, I needed to tell my mom's husband that I forgave him, that I was sorry about my mom. I just wanted to make everything as good as it could be. I couldn't apologize to my mom, but I could talk to him. More than anything, I hate when people are angry at me, and I hate being angry with people. It makes me feel anxious and sad. I would rather apologize for something I didn't do than have someone be mad. I would rather tell someone I forgive them and start over than feel angry. Maybe if I told him that I was sorry, he would say he was sorry; maybe I could find some sort of redemption through this, I thought. Maybe sitting in this church pew made me think he could find redemption, that I could find peace—that my mom was gone, but we didn't all need to suffer.

The priest I had talked to the day before walked to the front of the church in his white robe, starting the funeral, and my mind drifted, already worrying about how I was going to capture my mom during the eulogy and then realizing I wasn't even listening to the priest. Ten minutes into the service, my mom's husband wobbled in alone, walking down the main aisle of the church as the priest was talking. I watched as my grandma scooted to the side, making a place for him to sit next to her and my aunt who put her arm around him.

I felt sick. What was happening here? I was so sad about my mom, yet I still felt hurt by this. I was angry and confused, without the ability to understand every emotion I felt. I was angry that he was late for his wife's funeral and also angry that he was there at all. And suddenly I was OK with angry. I didn't want to say I was sorry to him, didn't want to forgive him, didn't want to look at him or be near him.

The priest never used the word *suicide* and didn't even allude to it during the service, nor did I expect him to. He talked of the usual themes of God calling us home. My sister and I, neither having spent much time in church in years, had resorted to Google to find our readings. When the priest had asked my sister if she had a suggested passage, Lisa told him she would get back to him. We both went on a hunt, wanting to find something that didn't feel too biblical, while acknowledging it actually had to be a reading from the Bible. We had teased each other with picking verses with names she wouldn't know how to pronounce, and settled on a verse known as one of the more poetic verses in the Bible, one that acknowledges grief and doesn't really provide an answer. This one felt honest, and didn't leave everything up to God, which neither of us were ready for.

My sister stood in front of the church and began: a reading from Lamentations.

My mom's sister and brother stood at the front of the church and told stories of when they all three were kids, taking turns in the story telling as if they had rehearsed it.

Theo, eleven, had asked if he could read something at the funeral. I had told him yes, thinking he would likely forget he asked, or see all the people and decide against it. But on this day, he wanted to speak and I walked with him to the lectern at the front of the church. He stood next to me and from the front pocket of his corduroy pants, he pulled out a piece of notebook paper folded five times into a tiny rectangle and slowly opened it. He rubbed his hand over the paper to smooth it out. His elfin handwriting in pencil filled eleven lines.

"My grandma," he began, in a voice louder than I expected.

He looked up toward his little sister, snuggled into her dad, and back down to the paper. He grabbed my hand. "She would ride the roller coasters with us, not because she wanted to, but because she wanted to make her grandchildren happy," he said. "She read *The Hunger Games* along with me so I wouldn't be scared. We all loved her very much."

He stayed next to me as I told a few stories about my mom, about how she always looked after us, about how she seemed constantly worried that someone was cold, and how she had knitted caps for her grandchildren when they were babies, even the summer babies in Phoenix, of how she collected socks for the homeless so their feet wouldn't be cold.

It was thirty-four degrees the morning my mom was found in the canyon. She had on a lightweight jacket.

"Mom," I said, "you weren't alone. You weren't. And I hope you were not cold in the end."

Theo and I walked back to our pew and sat down. The rest of the service was a blur, but I read the program—if that's what you call it—and Henry read a traditional verse from Romans that's often read at funerals about hope and trust in the Lord. We took Communion during the song "Here I Am, Lord," and I do remember squeezing my sister's hand as she walked back to her pew. I whispered, "I will raise you up on eagle's wings," which made her smile. She and I had discussed how the song had become an anthem at

Catholic funerals and that we couldn't have it at our mom's service. We teased each other that whichever of us died first, the other would insist the song be played at her funeral. It almost made me want to eat healthier and start running again.

The last song began, the recessional hymn, and it was supposed to be the Beatles' "Blackbird," my mom's favorite song. Instead, the music director led everyone in a gospel-like song called "River of Hope" with clapping, most of which was offbeat. My sister and I looked at each other, confused. Then we realized my aunt and grandma must have changed the last song, and all we could do was laugh. It was as if none of this could possibly be happening. It all seemed too absurd for reality. Had our mom really just died and now people were clapping and singing this song we had never heard? It may have been that we were so uncomfortable, so in shock and just tired and so sad, that all we could do was laugh.

As each person left the church, my mom's best friend, Ellen, handed them a piece of dark chocolate, my mom's favorite treat. It sat in my mouth taking forever to dissolve, like a Communion wafer. During the lunch and reception after the funeral, I fidgeted with the foil from the chocolate, folding it into a thin strip, as tiny as I could do with one hand in the pocket of the dress that Mom had bought me for my birthday the previous month.

That afternoon after the funeral, I was supposed to stop by my mom's house to see if there was anything there I wanted. My sister had told me to pick it out and she could box it up and send it to me. When I pulled up to the house alone, I saw the cactus garden my mom had just written to us about planting, the desert willow trees where she had hidden Easter eggs for my kids, the pear tree we had planted for Mother's Day two years ago, and then the big white pickup truck. The truck belonged to my mom's husband and its presence meant he was there. I couldn't go in, couldn't even turn the car off to stop and park. I didn't want to see the house again. I drove away, and left the next morning for Ohio.

When we got home to Cincinnati, one of John's family friends, a priest, called to check on me. We still had a landline and I pulled the cord with me as I sat on the kitchen tile to talk by the back door. He told me how sorry he was, wanting to know how I was doing, how the kids were. I didn't know him well, or really at all, but I knew he was close with John's family and they had sponsored him while he was in the seminary at Notre Dame.

I couldn't answer, not for myself and not for the kids. I'm not sure I even knew how we were doing; I was just so sad. I told him that I no longer believed in God and didn't believe in heaven, but he must, and so he must know. I could barely say anything else, but asked, "Father, is she OK?" I meant, is she in heaven?

"What?" he said. "Who?"

"Is she OK?" I repeated. "My mom. Is she OK? Is she in heaven?"

I could hear him take a deep breath.

"I don't know," he told me. "The truth is that we don't know with certainty what is next. I just have faith," he said. "We all just have faith."

I told him thank you.

"Take care of yourself," he said.

I pulled my knees into my chest and cried. Couldn't he have told me a story, told me she was at peace with a God she believed in?

That first week after we arrived home in Cincinnati, Henry, Luke, and Lucy each received a note in the mail from my mom. She must have mailed them just before she died. Since we had moved, my mom had sent cards and stickers in the past few months, silly presents from the dollar store like satin and felt leprechaun hats and colored beads, stretchy rubber bunnies and plastic eggs, clutter that got caught in the vacuum cleaner, that I simultaneously loved and hated. She sometimes didn't remember who she sent a card to, and sent doubles to one of the kids, and forgot another. Sometimes she mailed a card every day to each of them. The kids all loved getting mail, racing each other to the mailbox to see if there was a card with GRANDMA written in block-style writing in the left corner of envelopes and boxes, and checking to see which stamp she had used. Theo checked the mailbox for a week, looking for a card from my mom that never arrived.

My mom's husband died from a stroke three months later.

Chapter 3

A Cruel Summer

THE SUMMER AFTER my mom died seemed the most difficult. May of 2012 was a shuffle of kids' activities and John keeping things afloat at home, which meant I was, at best, going through the motions of life, of being a mom, of making dinner and doing laundry, of signing paperwork for four children's lives at school, of showing up at baseball games and lacrosse practice, and going to work full-time as an editor—but John was making all of the decisions. He scheduled the playdates and told me which game was at which time and where. Since our first was born, I had been the one who kept the calendar updated, the one who knew which child needs to see the dentist and which one needs an eye appointment, who needs their annual checkup and who needs a follow-up at the dermatologist. I was the one who remembered that after Tuesday night's baseball game we need to wash the baseball pants for the second game of the week on Thursday because it's another home game and that means only the gray pants will work. What I couldn't juggle in my head, I had in a spreadsheet for the after-school car pool pickup and for ballet, baseball, and soccer games.

Now this fell to John. I could do something if it was scheduled, written on a calendar, and then transferred to a daily list. But somehow it felt impossible at the time to make the decisions and make the list. I would GPS my way to baseball games with addresses in suburbs I had never heard of, barely knowing the street names, but turning left or right when the voice coming from the car speakers told me to. I watched from a corner of the bleachers where I didn't have to talk with the other moms or anyone, so I didn't have to force myself to smile or act as if everything was OK, didn't have to see the grandparents who came to games, wishing my mom were there yet again. Now I'm aware of what grief can do to people, how isolating it can be, and I hope I know how to help others, or at least understand and respect their pain. Back then, if you took the GPS away from me, I couldn't tell you where I was, much less feel my way home.

Even when I smiled or laughed, I felt so empty.

Life goes on after tragedy or grief, we know this, and being a parent reminds you of this. People talk about how cruel it seems that the world continues, the sun rises, stores open, people walk about unaware of what has happened in your life, and yet, we go on. There isn't the possibility of pulling the covers up and staying in bed when lunches need to be packed, rain boots need to be tracked down, children need to be walked to school, work needs to be done. There isn't the option of just staying home or taking time off when you have a job, especially a new one. So I just moved through it, with the momentum of life and its rush carrying me along. And now I think perhaps I was lucky to have all these things to do.

I don't remember a lot about that summer. I felt so low, and when you imagine how low that was, think lower and that is where I was. It was the sub-basement of feelings. I can remember the feeling of it, rather than the actual details, the feeling of being in a tiny boat with water coming through holes that weren't even apparent, and the constant feeling of trying to stay afloat. There was no shoreline to see, no thought of even looking for one. There was just the idea that every day felt as if it was a struggle to not drown, and often the feeling that I didn't even want to try. Now I look back at that time, to look for clues of what I missed, and I find a box of sympathy cards with images of beaches and rainbows, doves and lilies, that friends mailed to me, notes I scribbled to myself in a journal, sometimes of inspirational quotes or sayings ("This, too, shall pass") and other times just moods ("Rotten. Overwhelmed. Sad.") and a Mom's Day letter from Luke in which he wrote how much he liked that I came to all his baseball games and made him dinner every night. (I made dinner!) I read through notes and letters filled with complete love and kindness, grace and comfort, and feel overwhelmingly grateful. But most of it doesn't feel familiar to me; it's as if I'm looking at mementos from a life lived by someone else. There are photos—a Blue Jays game on a trip to Toronto, a lacrosse tournament in Columbus, lunch in the park with John, a roller-skating party with Lucy—but I don't remember being there. The body protects itself somehow, using all its energy simply to live, not to participate or, at times, remember.

In the beginning, when someone asked about my mom, I simply said she died. She was old enough that younger people didn't seem surprised, or didn't need a reason. I was forty-two so I wasn't a kid. My mom was sixty-six. A shoulder shrug and an "I'm sorry," and we could move on—it wasn't like I was an orphan. I am grown and have a husband, my own children, this is part of life. Sometimes people would ask if my mom had been sick for long, and that question was more difficult to answer. Yes, and no, I thought, but I'm not entirely sure. I sometimes just said yes. Often what followed would be: I lost my aunt, neighbor, fill in the blank, to cancer, too, which seems to be the presumed cause of death for almost anyone. I didn't correct them; I didn't want to. It was easier that way, and that is what I wanted, to not talk about it, to not acknowledge it, to miss her privately and secretly. Most of the time, as in the obituary I wrote that celebrated my mom's life, I neglected to mention how she died. I didn't want to tell people. Her suicide wasn't a secret, but it was a wound, and talking about it allowed people dangerously close to the darkest parts of myself, the parts where we felt like the same person. Me, my mom, myself.

I didn't want to tell people that I had decided I didn't belong here anymore either.

Chapter 4

The Fear: I Was Becoming My Mom

I REMOVED MY seatbelt while driving and sped toward a concrete underpass; I jumped up to grab the pipes in our basement to see if they were strong enough to hold me or if they would simply collapse if I hung myself from them. I didn't want anyone to know how close I was to the ledge.

If I started talking about my mom, I might share more of myself. If I ignored it, perhaps it wasn't true, I was OK, and in part because if I told anyone, I would have to do something, and at that point, I couldn't see a path to feeling better, but I could very clearly see a path out of the pain. To follow her.

Some friends knew how my mom had died. The concern took a familiar path from "I'm sorry" to questions of "Are you OK?" to "You are OK, aren't you?" and "Seems like you're doing great." I learned to pretend I was. It seemed to be the answer people wanted, and they seemed to feel better if I said I was doing fine. Also then I didn't have to say much. So it became best to comfort others in the months after my mom's death. To avoid the conversation altogether, I began to go out of my way to show them just how well I was, saying OK to enough that they wouldn't need to ask more. I hosted summer dinner parties on our backyard deck, and posted happy photos on Facebook of Reds games with the kids, of summer vacation at the south shore of Massachusetts, of books I was reading. If I was together enough to share my reading list and the photos of grilled corn we made, I was OK enough to continue to live, or at least not look for a way out. I looked for the good every day in everything. I thought if I told friends that I was OK often enough, it would be true.

Once a week on Saturdays for about six months, I ran nine miles, partly for the empty space, a place to be alone, to simply listen to my feet on the pavement, for the birds, wind, and cars. It would clear my head, I thought, and would help me prepare for a half marathon that I was going to run with friends the next year. I had trained for the half marathon earlier that year, but the race fell on the day after my mom's funeral.

But all running seemed to do was give me time to think and wonder what I could have done to help my mom. I would list the things I had missed, fixated on what I hadn't done or things I'd done wrong. I knew enough to know this wasn't healthy, so I decided to tick through the reasons why logically I should be happy, repeating them as my phone buzzed to signal that I had run another mile. It was like a mantra of sorts, something I memorized in order and repeated. Amazing kids. A good husband. An interesting job. My dog. My neighborhood. Good books. The next mile, I would add more things, becoming more specific: Lucy's ballet recital, the interesting Tudors and rare bungalows and other houses I ran past that felt nothing like the ranch homes where I grew up. The hydrangeas that thrive here. I began to try to remember them in the same order and repeat them to myself, sort of like the children's game where someone picks the letter *A* and a name and a place that starts with the letter *A,* and the next person takes *B* but repeats both, and so on through to *Z* and then start over again. By the end of the run, I could recite a list that reached more than thirty-five reasons why I should be happy, but I couldn't force myself to believe them.

It's a lonely place to be and I was angry at myself for not being able to find the joy my life had. I continued meeting with my psychologist and glossed over just how bad I was feeling, saying things I thought she needed to hear. I couldn't look her or anyone else in the eye and say I no longer wanted to live, even if it was true.

I was afraid to say it out loud, afraid that if I said it out loud it *was* true, afraid that if it was true, I would have to go to a rehab center, somewhere far away, afraid that I wouldn't be with the kids or John. I was afraid I was just like my mom yet I told myself I wasn't like her. If I continued to push the bad feelings to the back of my head, to look for good, maybe the sadness or emptiness would go away.

My psychologist explained that it wasn't necessarily my mom's death that made me depressed, but rather her death added stress, and stress releases a mix of chemicals in some people's brains. Genetics, family history, and other things doctors still don't understand can trigger it. My psychologist told me she wanted to talk with my primary care physician to prescribe an antidepressant for me. I didn't want to take it. I barely took vitamins and didn't even like Tylenol. I was afraid the medicine wouldn't let me feel anything anymore (which wouldn't have been bad), and I couldn't understand how it could work, or if it was worth it.

I understand it's a common feeling, this depression after losing someone, especially losing someone to suicide, yet it often feels impossible to share. It's raw and scary, and sometimes I felt selfish or indulgent. Was I that privileged to spend so much time worrying about how I didn't help my mom, worrying if I was responsible? My mom wasn't a child; she was an adult who made her own decision. Yet her death consumed me, not just as grief, but because it felt preventable, because I wanted to figure out if I could have done something different to save her. At the very least, I worried I was the one who had somehow pushed her over the edge.

I reluctantly began taking the medicine, but that summer remained rough and I didn't feel that going through the motions was enough anymore. The pain of my mom's death compounded by the guilt I felt was too much. I hadn't been taking the medicine long and it takes at least thirty days to help. Depression took hold in a way where everything felt as if it took so much effort. Everything I needed to do felt as if it took too many decisions and it wore me out. Making dinner became something that made me tired, and the decisions I had to make sound ridiculous now but seemed so important and urgent at the time. Should I turn the oven on first or should I start slicing the Brussels sprouts? Should I start the pasta before or after I sauté onions? This type of decision-making consumed my day from the moment I woke up (should I use body wash or the bar of soap?), through work, taking care of the children, and until I went to bed. It sounds crazy, but I learned that this is how depression can take over your life.

It wasn't always the profound sense of sadness, though that also was there, but it was the simple steady inability to function—the daunting feeling of making choices, most that didn't even matter, throughout the day, that paralyzed me. And it didn't feel as if it would go away; it felt as if that was who I had become.

Thinking of living that way, of taking so long to get ready to go somewhere that I no longer wanted to go, didn't seem worth it. I felt as if the kids would certainly be better without me. I was worried they were going to start noticing and worrying about me, or maybe they already were. It would be easier for John without me and for all of them. That felt as true as anything.

When things are bad, I always have a tendency to retreat, slowly, closing myself off. I couldn't talk to my dad, fearing he would hear the sadness in my voice. John had taken on enough.

My sister and I avoided each other except for polite conversations about our children by text. It was as if we couldn't bear to hear our mom's voice in the other, couldn't talk about how our mom died. So we stayed an arm's length apart. It was all we were capable of as we both tried to survive.

I missed my mom so much that it was a physical pain. My chest weighed down, breathing was hard work, my skin felt like I needed out, but I couldn't escape it. And the idea that I was responsible for my mom's death made me feel unable to live with myself. I couldn't fix it and I couldn't make the feeling go away. I tried to listen to my psychologist, to tell myself that it wasn't my fault, that my mom made her own decision, but I couldn't shed the regret. I wanted to escape myself and there wasn't a way.

I wrote notes to each of my children on little note cards that had illustrations of saguaro cacti on the front, to tell them how proud I was of them, how much I loved them. I wrote to John to tell him how sorry I was, and to say good-bye. I told them this wasn't about them, but about me. I wanted them to know that I understood they would be better off without me, that I wished I could fix it, but I couldn't, that it wasn't fixable. I told them I hoped that one day they would understand. I wanted the notes to be elegant and short, meaningful and helpful, something that might sustain them on the roughest days. I wrote and rewrote these notes on blank paper to copy into the cards, unhappy with my handwriting, or the way I made a cursive letter in a word, the way I crossed out something I hadn't phrased correctly. I wrote them again, and put them in my underwear drawer to revise again. I truly believed at the time that my children would be better off without me—it seemed so normal and obvious. The depression had taken over, and somehow my brain now was convincing me that illogical things were true. I believed my brain. I believed that the children would be better off without their mom, and maybe at that point they in fact would have been. What depression wouldn't let me see was that they needed their mom, but a healthy version of myself.

The depression that gripped me and made me want to kill myself also probably made it difficult for me to follow through with suicide. I wanted to die; I prayed every night to not wake up. If there was a God, and I didn't think there was, maybe she would do this one thing—if not for me, then to spare my family. Every morning I woke up disappointed that I was still alive. Couldn't God let me see my mom again to say I'm sorry, to have one more hug? But then I blamed myself and decided God would make me live, painfully, for eternity. Was I too lazy to actually kill myself, too depressed to follow through? Or just too overwhelmed by the decisions and logistics to make it happen?

As a writer, or just as a mom, I was never satisfied with the notes I wrote to my children and to John. Did I properly explain how much I loved them, or how sorry I was? Did I leave them good enough instructions—reminding John where the kids' Social Security cards were, that there were four dress shirts and his new gray suit at the dry cleaner to be picked up, or that the gravy boat for the china was in a cardboard box marked CHRISTMAS in the basement next to the yard tools? (And really, would he even ever want to use a gravy boat?) Did they know that the dog only eats a certain type of dog food or she gets sick? Did the notes seem too much like to-do lists and not enough about how much I loved them? Did they know how proud I was of them? Did they know the kindness and compassion I saw in them? How could one note convey everything my children meant? Did it need to? One thing about being a writer is that you never want your last words to be those you don't like. How could I properly tell them what I thought they needed to hear? I wrote and rewrote. Then I put the notes in my drawer, thinking they might be enough.

LATER THAT SUMMER, there became a point at which death seemed the only answer. It was stronger than it had felt earlier—it wasn't something I could just wish for, but something I needed to act on, to do something about. Suicide is so impossible to understand, and the only way to fully understand it is to be there yourself, at which point you aren't super able to explain it, or add insight. And for a moment, I no longer wondered why my mom did it, why she killed herself. I understood. It was the only way at that point that she knew not to feel pain, the only way she could see to escape it. It was the one way she could get away from herself.

I wanted to tell my mom I was sorry, I wanted to tell her I was not mad at her. I wanted to tell her I understood. I wanted to tell her again that I loved her. I wanted to see where she ended her life, and I wanted to end mine, too.

Maybe many of us are sometimes one step from the ledge. I came home from work early one afternoon that summer, logged on to the computer, and bought a one-way plane ticket to Phoenix for that night. I wanted to be with her in the canyon. I no longer wanted to feel the way I did, but I hadn't been able to find a way out of it. I no longer wanted to feel as if I disappointed my children and family each day. I no longer wanted to be myself.

There were no direct flights that day, but there was an early evening flight with a layover in Dallas that would work. I would arrive at night, but with the three-hour time difference from Cincinnati, I could rent a car and get to the Grand Canyon by midnight. I needed to do something at that moment, I needed to stop waiting, stop thinking, stop worrying and regretting. I needed to stop feeling. John and our kids would be better off without me, I thought.

I was crying and I just needed to leave the house, I needed to do something to get away from my brain, my thoughts.

They felt inescapable. I told my kids that I needed to get out of the house for a bit. They were used to me needing time alone—"Just a minute" I would call out from the bathroom, sitting on the rug, crying.

This time, though, Lucy asked if she could come with me. She didn't want to stay home "with all the boys," she said, a common request with three big brothers when the house felt too full of baseball stats, fantasy football leagues, or just plain sports talk. I told her she needed to stay home with her brothers and I asked them to look after her. They nodded and Luke grabbed her hand to take her upstairs. As I opened the front door to walk to the car, Theo stopped me. Did he know something? Had he sensed that this sadness was bigger than before—did my haste to get out of the house feel more urgent this time, my look more serious? Or was he just a kid watching his mom leave?

He didn't say a word, but handed me a note as I closed the front door. I tucked it into my purse without looking at it.

I drove away. I was not OK; I didn't even know what OK looked like from there. I don't think I knew if there was a way to get to OK, that it could be a possibility. I knew I needed to end these feelings of pain, of guilt. The only way to describe the feeling was that I felt as if I needed to get out of my own skin. I felt so uncomfortable, so sad, so useless.

I drove twenty minutes toward the airport, somehow already starting to feel better knowing that I had a plan, that I had asserted control, that I wouldn't feel awful forever, that I wouldn't keep causing harm to my family by merely existing. I could almost breathe. I couldn't see a path back to my kids or to happiness or just to normal, but I could see a path to ease myself and my family of this burden I was becoming or already was. I could see a way to escape, to make this pain go away, a way to feel useful again, simply by my absence.

I started thinking about my children, not in the abstract way, but about the way Lucy's hair smells like strawberry shampoo when she curls into me at night to read a book, about the way Luke tries so hard to not smile sometimes, but can't help it, and even a laugh escapes, the way Henry, our teenager, never seems too old for a hug, the way Theo often looks as if he isn't paying any attention, and then he shares the most perceptive observations about how his siblings are feeling. I started crying, the kind of crying that reaches the point where you can't quite breathe, and even though I wanted to die, I knew I couldn't be a safe driver.

The brain works in weird ways. I wanted to die, but I didn't want to cause a car accident and hurt someone else, so I pulled off the road into a parking lot of a huge strip mall with a grocery store and spaces that extended for blocks, put the car in Park, and just sat. I felt I understood how my mom had felt on her last day. I felt almost a sort of calm take over. I was in control—I had made decisions and was following through. It was a control I never felt I had as a teenager when my stepfather abused me. I was no longer incapable of making a plan, but was able to think and take the steps to reach what I needed. I had made a decision just like she had. The pain that paralyzed me was going to end.

I knew I couldn't drive. I couldn't go home. I needed it to all be over. But first could I just stop crying so I could drive? I reached into my purse for a tissue and with it, I pulled out the note from Theo. It was written on a three-by-five-inch index card, narrow light blue lines on one side.

The other side was blank except for words written in a fuchsia fine-point Sharpie.

"I know U love me and I love U. Theo."

Theo, I thought, sweet Theo. He shouldn't have had to write this. He was only eleven.

A tiny bit of clarity poked through and I cried even more: I thought, I can't do this.

I could see my mom in Lucy, in her profile, in her cornflower-blue eyes that match my mom's, in the way she stands just like me and just like my mom, one foot turned in, the other straight ahead, a strange genetic connection, or just a learned mannerism passed down through two generations. Even at five, Lucy has the same closeness with me that I had with my mom, unnaturally so, perhaps, or maybe just perfect. I missed my mom in ways that physically hurt, but I carried parts of her—the way no one could tell our voices apart when we answered a phone, our shared love of handwritten notes, and a love for our children that is impossible to bend. And, I realized, there she was, right in front of me, in Lucy, my daughter who shared so much with my mom, even that same compassionate heart. If you ever told Lucy that anyone was sick or injured, she would remember to ask about them when you mentioned them again even if it was days or months later—she wanted to make sure they were better.

I could not let Lucy become me. I could not have her feel everything I had felt because I missed my mom so much. I could not have Henry, Theo, and Luke feel this way, too. I could not let them become me. I needed to live through this. I needed to for them, and for me.

I drove home. Maybe out of fear, or maybe relief, I didn't

tell anyone I had bought the plane ticket. I never boarded the plane.

It would be poetic and beautiful to say that Theo's note was the turning point and that I was magically healthy after that day. This is a book, but it's not fiction. So instead this day was a reminder that I mattered, that I was needed, and for some reason, I could begin to see this more clearly. It is also possible that the antidepressants I had been taking were beginning to take hold. This note from Theo was my reminder, something physical, something tangible I could look at when I couldn't see the truth on my own.

I carried the note in my wallet. I returned to therapy, deciding I didn't want to die, but I hadn't quite decided I wanted to live, either. Would this be the condition in which I would live? It was closer to where I wanted to be, but if I was going to stay here on earth and live, I needed to do something more.

When I first met with my psychologist in Cincinnati, I had been afraid that if I told her the truth—that I just wanted the pain and guilt to go away, and that the only way I could see out of it was death—she would try to talk me out of it. I worried that if I told her the truth, she might need to have me evaluated by psychiatrists at a hospital. And there was no way I could pass an evaluation that would say I was safe. I would have been declared a danger to myself. I wasn't sure I wanted help at that point and my mind had raced: I needed to finish editing a story, to get Lucy to ballet class, the boys to a baseball or lacrosse practice. No one had made dinner. I still needed to find a dentist. I didn't have time to be evaluated, didn't have time to make space in my head to figure things out. Maybe I have always been a danger to myself at some point, maybe not for death, but definitely for reckless activities—from cutting myself in high school to anorexia, both common coping mechanisms for victims of sex abuse. Maybe everything I had been doing my whole life had come to a head right there, forcing me to deal with all of it.

I needed to be OK, and maybe the fact that I realized this, that I knew I wanted to finish editing a story, that I knew I wanted to be home to make dinner, that I knew I wanted to take Lucy to ballet, that theoretically I wanted to make dentist appointments for the kids, meant that I wanted to live. It meant I had things to look forward to, things that mattered. Perhaps I didn't need an important declaration or will to live—I just needed to want to get to the next thing.

Maybe this "one day at a time" philosophy wasn't just baloney, or inspirational messages on Instagram posts, but actual advice that made sense. When I woke up, I couldn't think all the way to dinner. Instead, I would tell myself, think that you want to walk the kids to school. After you do that, think about how you would like to go have lunch with John at your favorite Vietnamese sandwich shop, and then think about a story you are excited to work on with a reporter, and then you can think about finally sitting around the dinner table with your family, together. And somehow it would become a day, a good day. All of it was overwhelming, but I would take it in steps, segments. I didn't set myself up for an impossible task of waking up in the morning and saying: Make this a great day. I looked just to the next thing. Maybe this couldn't be a sustainable strategy, but perhaps it could get me to the next place I needed to be.

So this time I knew I needed to tell my psychologist the

truth, even if she had already suspected it. I needed to not just admit it, but confront it.

I carried Theo's note in my purse as a reminder. I lived in fear that I was going to turn into my mom. I worried my depression would mimic hers, even if I didn't truly understand hers, except how things had ended. I worried my children and my sister's four children would also be at higher risk. Would we be? I began to think that the more I knew, not just about my mom's suicide, but about suicide in general, would be good. Not just the person who died, but those left behind.

And so I told my psychologist that I had wanted to kill myself.

"You said 'had wanted,' " she said. "Do you still feel that way now?"

"Not now," I said, telling the truth.

"And what if that changes?" she asked.

"I know what to do," I said. "I'm no longer afraid."

"So what will you do?" she asked. "You need to make sure that you have a safety plan in place."

I understood that because I had been depressed, and considered suicide, I needed a plan, one that I knew I could do if I fell back into depression. I understood it might happen, but that it wouldn't be a disaster if it did. Sometimes getting better isn't a straight upward line. It can become a place of caution and checklists. A place where I know not to stay alone in my head too often so that my mind is too busy to be left alone, to know that sometimes even when I'm surrounded by people but I'm still lonely, I need to make myself stay there anyway, to say "yes" always to walking the dog with my best friend even if all I want to do is sit on my heating vent with a book, to make myself take a yoga class each week, to invite people at work for coffee, to connect even if it's only online, to find something new each week—a piece of art, a restaurant, the tall windows of a building I never noticed before—to put my feet on the actual earth and feel the grass, something that makes me happy I'm alive besides all of the obvious reasons. I also need to know when I need time to myself, that sometimes a day of talking to people all day is too much, that I need a break. I accepted the increased risks, and decided to try to guard against it.

My psychologist could see very quickly that I was both succeeding and failing, that I was both strong and fragile. She listened, she asked questions. I cried and told her how I felt, but I often punctuated every sentence with, "I'm OK!"— perhaps the best sign that someone is not OK. She wrote things down. I often wondered if I bored her as I droned on about how sad I was, about how hard the daily tasks that most people don't even think about in life had become for me, and was she taking notes about me or working on a novel or making her to-do list? It was embarrassing how tired it made me to sit on a couch and talk for an hour.

People who have never gone to see a therapist may not understand how draining it can be to talk about things you haven't before, or how tiring it can be to simply share the worst parts of yourself. John would ask how my session was when I came home each week, wanting to know what we had talked about and what I learned. He was showing his support, but I often would tell him I couldn't talk about it and didn't want to talk about it. It was enough to talk about it once; I didn't feel like then doing it again.

Still, I returned week after week. She once said to me: "There is a feeling that sometimes you are depressed because your life is depressing." Dealing with my mom's suicide and the repressed trauma from the sex abuse both were pretty depressing. "But there seems to be something more here," she said, "and maybe you needed help a long time ago, and maybe it's grown worse with your mom's death, but I can tell you that you will feel better one day."

I wasn't sure if psychologists were allowed to say that, sort of like doctors telling a cancer patient they will get better when how could they possibly know? But she could see the progress I couldn't see. She could see the medicine, therapy, and work beginning to bring me back. And what I needed at that time was to hear someone tell me I was getting better, could get better, that this wasn't permanent, that things would change. It was difficult to see or believe that on my own.

I have been asked how I climbed out, how I am here, or rather, why I am here, and the short answer is a lot of therapy, good people, and medicine.

Sometimes, it seemed, I just needed something to get me to the next thing. In the beginning, when things were very bad, it helped to carry Theo's note in my wallet so I could look at it during the day. In the worst times, I was lucky that I had friends who texted just to check in, and a husband who knew to send a kid with me on errands so I wouldn't be alone. When people ask me, I tell them that the actual story of getting better feels monotonous and boring and doesn't follow a straight line, that I would feel better and then not, hitting a setback. My medicine was adjusted, changed, stopped when I thought I was better and didn't need it, and then restarted again. I tell people that getting better really was walking the kids to school, and then looking forward to petting the dog when I got home, and then knowing I would see the gorgeous oak trees in the neighborhood as I drove to work, and then that I would have interesting conversations with reporters at the newspaper and stories to edit, and then find something to continue to look forward to, even if it meant a day where I had to look forward to something almost every hour. And sometimes I was so tired of myself that I didn't want to think about it anymore, didn't want to think about myself, my mom, or suicide, and that was allowed. I needed a break from myself at times.

And then some days, I wondered why I was here. This was different from when I asked this same question as a child, or a college student, or even when I was worried about my rightful place on the planet. The questions felt different this time—it was about me, but also her: "Why am I here and she is not?" "What is it about my mom that made her lose her strength, her will to live, her love for life and curiosity of the world when somehow mine remained, or something remained enough?" And the real answer is that I'm not entirely certain why I am here instead. I wish I knew, that psychologists and scientists who study the brain knew, that they better understood suicide. I know there are days when the feeling of hopelessness, sadness, and defeat returns. But I do now understand that it isn't permanent, that the feelings visit rather than stay. And I know it now, instead of not knowing or not being able to differentiate a temporary feeling from one that won't go away, that clings to you in a way that makes you want to crawl out of your own skin to rid yourself of it.

And so getting better started with wanting to get better or being pushed to get better, including by my husband who wouldn't let me make any excuses about why I was tired of going to counseling, how tired I was of myself, of talking, or just how tired I was. "Let's get up, let's go for a walk," he would say. And so I went.

Sometimes the routine of therapy was therapeutic enough, something I had to do, so that on Tuesdays I would leave work early and become part of the traffic headed to the suburbs, eleven miles on the freeway, past the dog kennel on the left to an industrial office park where three doors down the hallway my psychologist had a room so messy it made me uncomfortable. I spent the first part of each of our sessions tidying her office in my head, restacking the books into piles by size and color on the bookshelves, folding the blankets that lay haphazardly across the couch, mentally throwing out the three extra chairs that made the office feel cramped, and tossing out some of the papers I thought must have been gathering there since her doctoral dissertation days. My mind straightened the photos on the walls, where frames never lined up right, took away the six or more mismatched coffee cups, and then I tried to simply focus on her questions about myself and about my mom.

One day when my anxiety about my mom's death and the role I feared and believed I had played was making it difficult for me to even sit still on the couch, she asked a question.

"Tell me what you knew then," she said.

"What do you mean?" I asked.

"Tell me what you knew in the month before your mom died. Not what you know now or what you learned afterward."

"I don't know," I said. "My mom was sad. She would talk, but sometimes she felt far away. She felt empty when I talked to her. She was there, but not."

I tried to explain it in a way that didn't sound cliché. My mom felt hollow—her words were coming out, but they were just words.

"Yes," she said. "Did you know she was sick?"

"It's so obvious now, isn't it?" I told her.

"Not what you know now," she said. "Then, think back to then."

It was impossible for my brain to put itself back into that time. I didn't want to; every time I started to think about it, I felt terrible. I thought about what I would have done then with what I knew now, with who I am, what I saw, what could have been. I thought about all the things I wanted to say to my mom, that I would have gone to her wherever she was, to let her know she was needed, loved. I couldn't go back to that spot in time. I could only see what I know now, what I have read, what I knew, what I felt, what had happened. It made me feel guilty.

My psychologist decided I needed something more to help.

"Have you ever done EMDR?" EMDR is short for *eye movement desensitization and reprocessing*. I had, actually. My psychologist in Phoenix had suggested we use EMDR to talk about repressed memories of sexual abuse. She had explained that some psychologists use it to help people process traumatic memories. There's conflicting research on whether it's helpful, but some believe it might be particularly helpful with people suffering from post-traumatic stress disorder. It sounded crazy to me, but it turned out to be helpful in understanding the abuse and better understanding that it wasn't my fault. EMDR is a process that uses rapid eye movement while a person discusses painful memories. The idea, very loosely, is that as your eyes follow a light or sound, it helps your brain better process trauma in a safe environment and a healing process can begin.

Now, part of my current therapist's goal was to replace the negative memory I had about myself—because I had not spoken up about the sex abuse at the time, and because of how I had missed signs of ways to help my mom—with a more positive belief such as: I am now in control of my life.

"Let's try," she said.

She handed me two clickers to hold, one in each hand. She turned on a thin bar with tiny lights along it. She set it on a table. My eyes, she explained, were to follow the light. The light moved back and forth and my eyes moved back and forth and tracked it and my hand used the clicker when the light hit that side. The light moved back and forth, my eyes tracked, and my hands clicked as I watched. It was hypnotic and soothing. My brain couldn't wander. My eyes moved back and forth, back and forth, and I was thinking about nothing but the lights.

"Tell me about you and your mom," she said.

"We were close," I said. "So close that sometimes my husband would be irritated by our closeness. I never wanted to hurt my mom's feelings, always wanted to include her. Sometimes he would tell me that my family was now the six of us. 'Yes, she is your mom, but you are too close.' "

"Tell me why that is," she said.

"I still felt like I needed to take care of her, even when I was married, even when I had kids. I had needed my mom to be happy. If she was happy, selfishly, I would be happy. I think children seem to know this. I knew this. I knew this as a child. If she was happy, I was happy. I never shook that feeling."

"So when you told her about the abuse, she stayed with her husband," she said.

"Yes."

"And how did that feel?"

"Wrong," I said. "It felt awful."

"Follow the lights," she said.

I didn't cry, my eyes followed the lights.

"It was hard to see, to reconcile, that she stood by him. I was angry. But I was afraid to tell her I was angry. At that time, mostly what my mom and I talked about were the facts—"here is what happened"—not how it made me feel, not how it made her feel. She didn't ask. I didn't tell her how I felt. And I didn't ask how she felt. I never asked."

I said I moved to Ohio before we resolved things—the distance between us grew, physically, of course, but more. We talked, but not about feelings.

"So, I asked you to write her a letter, right?" she said.

"Yes."

"Why is that?"

"Remind me," I said.

My eyes continued to follow the lights and the messiness of her office faded away.

"So you could tell her how you felt, so you could try to end this gap," she said.

I had told her that my mom and I hadn't been able really to talk much of late. I updated my mom on the kids, and our new house, my job, but something was missing between us.

We had both tried to be polite, not wanting to upset the other one, so most of our conversations had been about anything but us, our relationship, and this secret. Our conversations could be choppy, starting with the idea that it might work, one of us would recount her day devoid of emotion, trying so hard not to upset the other one that nothing was said. But until something was said about it, we would remain distant. There would be nothing.

We both were going through a very difficult time, but weren't sharing this with the other. We wanted to protect each other—we didn't want the other to worry.

"I couldn't say anything. I didn't want to hurt her. Didn't want her to feel worse."

"So what did you want to tell her?"

"I wanted her to know what happened with her husband," I said.

"Your stepdad?"

"My mom's husband, yes," I said, folding my legs up under me on the couch.

"But you never call him that. You never refer to him as your stepdad."

"Well, I never did. Even before this. I had a dad. My mom's husband had his own children. He was my mom's husband, not my dad. I was a teenager when I met him. So he wasn't like a dad."

"OK, go on," she said.

"So, I wanted her to know what he did. But more than that, I wanted her to understand why I did what I did. Why I didn't tell her, and for her to understand why it was so hard for me to see her take care of him, for her to choose him, maybe, over me."

"Is that what you think? That she chose him?"

"Maybe," I said, trying to figure out if I was embarrassed, and feeling like I did when my dad left our family when I was a child, that he was choosing his new girlfriend over us. I felt abandoned, not chosen again.

"What did you want her to know?"

"That it happened. And I didn't want it to happen. I was so afraid of her finding out, of knowing, of being mad at me."

"Do you think she knew?"

"No," I said, starting to cry.

"Do you think it seems possible that she couldn't have known?"

"I don't think my mom's brain would allow for something so awful to have happened.

"I just wanted her to be happy. I just wanted her happy. I didn't remember her happy when I was a kid. My mind skipped all the good parts of growing up, but it found all of her sadness, all of the times she seemed empty. My mom had been unhappy for so long. He made her happy. He did. So I had to make her happy, too."

I paused. Because I couldn't breathe, because my eyes were following the lights, thinking back to all the nights when I counted backward by tens, when I didn't make a sound because I didn't want her to come in and what if she somehow thought I wanted this?

"So you did anything to protect her then?"

"Yes."

"So when your mom found out, she didn't believe you, right?"

"No. She didn't. But then she did. I told her I was sorry.

She said she felt like she never could make it up to me. How sorry she was that I had lived with that, that I hadn't told anyone. I told her she didn't need my forgiveness. There was nothing to forgive. She didn't know. She did the best she could at the time."

"So is this what you wanted her to know?"

"Yes."

"So you wrote it. But you didn't know what she was going through. You only knew what you were going through. And she only knew what she was going through."

We talked a little longer, my eyes following the light, putting myself back in that moment, how I felt.

I had drafted a letter to my mom. I had given it to my therapist on a Monday at our weekly session and had asked her to read it. I trusted that she would know if it was right, if it expressed what we had talked about over so many hours of therapy. I wanted my mom to know everything about how I felt, what she meant to me—I wanted her to know so much that she could have heard me talking with my therapist about.

My therapist had said the letter could help my relationship with my mom, that if we couldn't have the conversation on the phone, this letter would let my mom really see and not just hear how I felt, that I didn't blame her, how I loved her, how I wanted her here.

I had thanked her for the session. And I emailed that letter on Tuesday.

On Thursday, my mom jumped into the canyon.

Chapter 5

Learning to Understand Suicide

MY BRAIN FELT equally consumed with grief as with a deep curiosity to better understand suicide, of how to think about it or even talk about it myself. Before my mom died, suicide had felt distant; I had never lost anyone even remotely close to me to suicide. The one place that had really made me think about the issue of suicide was in journalism.

In 2013, almost one year to the day after my mom killed herself, I was sitting at my desk in the newspaper office in Cincinnati reviewing the headlines and analyzing which stories were doing well online. There was a preview for a Reds game that night, a city council discussion about preserving a historic building (which you could probably find almost any week in a midsize Midwest city trying to both move forward and save its history). It was a fairly normal day, a Monday with the perfect kind of spring weather and a clear blue sky, a day when the temperature would hit sixty-three.

"Shots fired at La Salle," I heard one of the reporters say.

In a newsroom, reporters almost always listen to a scanner, a radio that allows you to hear police and fire department actions in real time, learning where and why crews are dispatched. Much of it is routine, and as a reporter you learn to half-listen to the constant chatter, of stalled cars blocking a lane on a busy road, someone with trouble breathing, a report of a suspicious person near a house. And you also learn that some things require you to listen closer. A report of gunshots usually perks up a reporter to listen to what's coming next—the location, if anyone was hit, whether there was more than one shot fired. The police scanner is the background noise of many newsrooms. La Salle is a school, a Catholic all-boys' school on the west side of town, and reports of shots fired at a school grabbed everyone's attention.

"Roll. Now," one of the online news producers said. "We'll update you on the way." A photographer and reporter ran to the door, took the elevator down nineteen floors, jumped in their car, and drove to the school. The photo editor—always the best and fastest in a newsroom because they know a photographer can't miss a shot, but a reporter can interview enough people after the fact to write a story—began redirecting photographers on other assignments toward the school. The adrenaline moved some quicker—it could be a big story.

I immediately felt worried and dreaded that this might be another mass school shooting; it was only a few months after Sandy Hook, but before Parkland and Santa Fe. School shootings were frequent enough that you no longer were surprised when the next one happened. After twenty six- and seven-year-old students and six teachers and staff members were shot and killed at Sandy Hook, we realized that shootings could happen anywhere. I just hoped it wouldn't be in my city.

At first I felt quietly thankful that this shooting wasn't at either of the schools where my children attended, that they were safe, not hiding behind a locked door in a supply closet somewhere. I felt selfish about my first thought and started walking around the newsroom to see who might know someone with kids at La Salle, or who had kids at La Salle. While Cincinnati had grown to more than two million people over the past decade, the region still can feel quite small and insular. People in Cincinnati still ask, "Where did you go to school?" after meeting someone new, and they don't mean college, they mean high school. It seems everyone is separated by only two or three degrees, with people connecting after only a few questions, especially according to high schools. It generally keeps the city polite, and people are less likely to say anything bad about someone else, because it's possible they know them through a cousin, a work friend, or high school. This city identity is strong, and I knew it would be useful as we tried to find someone who could tell us something.

Within minutes, one of the reporters had reached a mom who had already talked to her son who attended La Salle. She told us that yes, her son said that a gun had been fired on campus, but this was not a school shooting the way we typically think of them. Yes, there was a student in a classroom with a gun, and at least one shot was fired. But in this case, it seemed, the teenager didn't point the gun at anyone else, no students or teachers. Instead, a teenage boy stood at his desk in a computer lab, put a gun to his temple, and fired.

I felt shattered. He was just a kid; I thought about how

alone he must have felt, even while he was in a room with so many others; how when you are a teenager, things can feel so big because problems consume a larger portion of your life. Even in my deepest sadness about my mom's suicide, I knew that true tragedy comes when children kill themselves. There aren't sadness Olympics, of course, but I think that nothing can be worse than losing a child, and nothing worse than losing them to suicide.

"What do we do?" the online producer asked. She was texting with the reporter who was talking with students and family just outside the school gates. The producer gathered notes and tried to decide what we could write and post on-line. "It's looking like a suicide."

But we didn't have this confirmed yet; all we had from police was that there was only one victim and he had been transferred to the hospital. We had the other details from the mom of one of the students, and from students who shared what they knew.

We don't write about suicides, I thought. I knew this as one of the first rules of journalism, engrained in me as deeply as the Five W's and an H—the who, what, when, where, why, and how for telling a story. Not covering suicides wasn't something I was taught in journalism school, but it was something I learned along the way. I thought back to my first days of reporting when one of the assistant city editors leaned over to me from her desk and said, "We don't cover suicides."

It was in 1993, and I had just started my first full-time newspaper job after graduating from college in Northern California. After sending my résumé to editors at more than seventy-five newspapers, I wound up in Albuquerque, New

Mexico. I was hired to work the five A.M. shift for the afternoon newspaper, meaning I mostly covered crime and then really anything else that happened before the afternoon reporter replaced me around three that afternoon—restaurant openings, school awards, fires. The afternoon papers were sort of the first iteration of the internet and online news, a place where news that occurred in the morning was reported and where stories from the morning paper were updated and published in one edition in the late morning and another by early evening, dropped on doorsteps before dinner.

"Except," she said.

Except—there's always an *except*.

"Except if it's a famous person or if the suicide stops traffic or something, we don't cover people who commit suicide," she told me, in the same factual tone she had told me which desk at the county jail was where I checked bookings, and which basket to place my time card in on Fridays. Not covering suicides was an unwritten rule and I had believed it for years without question.

As a young reporter that first summer I worked for *The Albuquerque Tribune,* I had heard on our police scanner that a teenager had been shot. It was late afternoon and it was an hour past the time I should have gone home, but I was finishing a story for the next day's paper. There had been a fifteen-year-old girl shot once in the head. She was dead.

"Take the phone," my editor said, "and roll."

Editors liked to say "roll," which to a new reporter made things seem more exciting and important, but mostly it made them seem super urgent.

I signed the logbook to check out the newsroom's new

mobile phone, as big and as heavy as a brick, which rested in a special briefcase and offered a belt as one way to transport it. I carefully put the phone in the front seat of my car, thinking the phone likely cost more than my old Honda, and briefly considered buckling the seatbelt around it. I drove to a trailer park in the southernmost tip of the city down a gravel road and found one mobile home surrounded with yellow caution tape and more cop cars than I had ever seen in one place. I got out and checked in with the sergeant on duty. I could see a teenage boy staring straight ahead, no crying, just sitting in the back of a police car.

A few neighbors watched out their front windows, so I began to knock on doors. No one answered at the first two, even though I knew someone was home. At the third house, a woman opened the door and stared. I asked her if she knew anything about the teenage girl who lived across from her. She told me she didn't, but that she had heard a shot.

"Just one?" I asked.

"Yes. And I know gunshots. We hear them around here some nights, so I know that's what it was."

She told me she didn't want to give her name, and she really hadn't told me anything so I didn't need it anyway, but I said I understood and thanked her for her time, and for opening her door. She smiled and closed the door.

I walked over and waited with reporters from three TV news stations and the night cops' reporter from the morning newspaper whom I worked with when I had been a news intern the previous summer.

"Might be a long night," the reporter told me. He'd been a reporter for as long as I'd been alive, and a good mentor the past summer. Practical with his advice, never flustered, but also someone who liked carrying a police scanner and his own brick phone strapped to his belt, he still loved covering crime. We waited while the TV reporters did live shots for the six o'clock news, pointing to the police tape and mobile home. I thought about the girl who was inside, if the boy in the police car had killed her, or if maybe he had simply been the one who discovered her.

I was only seven years older than the dead girl inside that house.

By seven that night, the police sergeant met us at the edge of the yellow caution tape.

"Suicide," he said.

I looked around to see the reaction of the veteran reporters, those who weren't at one of their first shootings, the ones who were comfortable standing behind police tape, the ones who didn't seem sad and afraid knowing a teenage girl was just feet away, dead. I noticed they stopped listening after he said "suicide." I took their lead, as I saw them folding up their tripods and putting gear away to leave. I took the phone from my belt, which at that time hung heavy on my frame, and called the night editor.

"Suicide," I told her.

"Go home, kid," she said. "See you tomorrow."

Reporters from the TV stations packed up and left, too.

BUT ON THIS morning in Cincinnati about twenty years later, one of the online producers yelled to me, "We've got the boy's name now." And I was no longer the reporter, but a mom who was thinking about this teenage boy, of his parents, if he had a brother or a sister. The producer had been texting with one of the reporters who was standing on a street near the school, and said that the school had already changed the marquee on the front of the school to read: PRAYERS FOR [THE BOY'S NAME]. A few students and parents had confirmed it.

"Do we go with it?" another asked.

The question of reporting and writing about suicide on this day felt different. As the managing editor at *The Cincinnati Enquirer*, I oversaw breaking news and digital news, which for better or worse is often posted seconds after we learn something, as we try to discern what's true and what isn't, what we need to publish on the news site so people know, and because I know we don't want to get beat by the competition.

But I also know that being first isn't better than being right.

I thought back to January of 2011, when U.S. Representative Gabrielle Giffords was shot during a meeting with constituents held outside a Safeway store in her district in Tucson. I was working as an editor in Phoenix at that time. My friend, who would later come work with me as the sports editor in Cincinnati, was editing the home page, meaning he was the one who would decide what news was ready to share, and what could wait, which headline to write and where to place it. In those first seconds, the police scanner chatter said that the representative had been shot in the head. Another dozen people had been shot and some were dead at the scene. We didn't have many details. We had reporters, including my husband, driving to Tucson, where we didn't have any reporters based.

National Public Radio had reported that Rep. Giffords

died. And NPR wasn't looked at as a news organization that posted things early. They were thorough, thoughtful, and reserved. Editors were yelling to the home page editor, to the room, "We've got reports she's dead. Post. NPR is reporting it."

But my friend held back.

"We need to wait," he said. "We haven't confirmed this. I don't care that it's NPR. We haven't confirmed it." Other outlets said Rep. Giffords was dead and attributed this fact to NPR. The editor waited for updates from our reporters. Giffords was still alive.

In the newsroom in Cincinnati, I thought, We have to do this right. We can't publish anything we don't know for certain.

"Wait on the boy," I said.

This is all we knew for certain: A shot had been fired in a classroom. One teen was transported to a hospital. There was a flurry of reporters from four TV stations reporting on this shooting in Cincinnati. None of them said it was a suicide, none of them said the boy's name. We knew there was a student. We knew he had a gun. We knew only one person had been shot. We believed he shot himself. The boy, I realized, was only a few years older than my eldest son at the time, who was sitting safely in a classroom a few miles from my office.

We posted a story on our news site, but it had few details. I was hesitant to add more—I wanted to do this right. We needed to learn everything about this teenager and the shooting. Were students in his class, at the school, in danger? There was a kid in a classroom with a gun, so likely at least twenty other children were also in the class. How would

I feel if one of my children were in the classroom when this happened? Would I deserve to know who brought the gun to the class? Would I need to know this information from the newspaper? Would I need to know who potentially put my child at risk? Would I need to know right then? And what if my kid wasn't in the class? Did I need to know? The questions bounced around in my head as the producer asked me again, "Should we go with the kid's name? Should we use the photo of the marquee with his name?"

"No," I said. "Not now."

We could not publish the name of the boy, for many reasons—but then, I justified, we didn't have confirmation strong enough to report. And he was only seventeen.

In the following hours, police confirmed that the boy had tried to kill himself. We learned the boy's name from several places including unofficially from a police source and from several families. We learned that the boy was at his desk with a .45-caliber semi-automatic gun and there were twenty-two students and a teacher in the room with him. Our story online said all of this, but didn't name the boy. Our newspaper's editor wanted to run the name. The teen had put students at risk, which she argued outweighed his privacy. People at the school knew who he was. His name had been on social media, she said.

I wanted to tell her that this boy was still a juvenile, a kid really, that no other students were harmed, that maybe the parents in the class had the right to know who he was, but that no one else did. If we were lucky, I thought, the kid would live and this would be but a blip in a long and happy life. My mind drifted back a year earlier, to the moment I saw my mom's name in a story online in my hometown newspaper that suggested her death was a suicide. It was a few days after she had died and the headline WOMAN WHO DIED AT CANYON ID'D was placed under the tab labeled "Most Read" on azcentral.com.

When I worked at azcentral.com, the news site where stories from *The Arizona Republic* newspaper appeared, stories about deaths and suicide at the Grand Canyon were a curiosity. Even if you hadn't visited the canyon, you knew so much about it and people read these stories, a lot of people. They clicked on the headline even if the story said little more than someone's name, when they died, and an updated number of the people who had died at the canyon that year. I wondered if I had run any of these types of stories when I worked at the newspaper. Had I run anyone's name? Had I written a brief like this on one of my weekend shifts when I made calls to the county sheriffs' departments around the state to learn of any news? It made me feel sick to think that I might have, just as seeing my mom's name in the newspaper had made me feel sick that day. The article about her said it was a possible suicide. It felt like this detail should be private, ours to hold on to for a while alone. It wasn't that I felt ashamed, a feeling that surrounds some families with suicides, but it felt invasive. It felt like our story, our pain, not something to share. She hadn't harmed anyone. Was the story any better by printing my mom's name? Or was it enough to say that a woman died at the Grand Canyon, and say her age, without saying her death had been suspected a suicide?

In Cincinnati, I recused myself from the decision of naming the teenager who fired the gun in the classroom. I couldn't think it through without thinking of my mom, of learning about her suicide, of having to tell others, of seeing it in print in the newspaper before I could even try to understand what had happened. I realized that I had been outranked by the editor of the newspaper, so maybe the decision was never mine to make. But I knew that my background might have made me sensitive, too sensitive, to make the decision, or maybe just the right amount of sensitive, actually, to make it.

I understand, the editor said.

Our newspaper published the teen boy's name.

And maybe we did the right thing.

Maybe the public's right to know outweighed his privacy, but that boy was seventeen. A month later, one of the TV news stations reported that the teen had moved from the hospital to a rehab facility. They didn't name him, didn't say much about his condition, other than that he had been moved. I've thought about this boy over the years, typically near the anniversary of my mom's death, even now, almost eight years later. I wonder: Did he survive? Is he healthy? How much does he remember from that day? He would be twenty-five now, and seventeen would seem like a lifetime ago, and while the shooting definitely changed the course of his life, I don't want it to define him. Is he glad he's alive today—is he glad he was saved? I read somewhere that the majority of people who attempt suicide and live are relieved to be alive, grateful they didn't die. I want to hug him, I want him to be OK. I want it to be his story to tell, if and when he's ready.

I wonder if the choice we made in not writing much about the suicide was right. Maybe if we had written more about the shooting and the potential mental health issues that teenagers face, we could have helped lessen the stigma around suicide. But he was a kid and his parents didn't want to talk, and had released a statement: "We thank all of you for your thoughts and prayers. We ask that the media please respect our privacy at this time so we can do what we need to do for our son and our family. We also ask that friends of our son and family please refrain from Facebook and Twitter comments. We appreciate the heroic efforts of UC Medical Center staff as they care for our son."

Without his parents or the boy himself talking with a reporter, the story felt like an invasion. I felt an obligation to protect the boy and his family, in part because I couldn't protect my mom or my family when she had died.

Many researchers and psychologists will say that destigmatizing suicide can lead to fewer deaths, that talking about it, writing about it, making the discussion of mental health issues a part of our conversation, will help. But another researcher has noted that there's never been a time when suicide was less stigmatized, yet our suicide rates are higher than they've ever been. Another asks, but what would the rates be if we didn't talk about it, how much higher might they be? I don't know the answer. But now, I wanted to shield this boy and his family. The next story about the boy withheld his name.

There remains a delicate balance in writing and telling stories about suicide. How we share these stories can shape how the public feels, reacts, and deals with suicide, from funding suicide research to the language we use when talking about it. It can shape if and how we talk about suicide in our homes and schools. The media's enormous responsibility has evolved over the years.

We know the media can play a key role in helping us and our society both talk about suicide and understand it. This means how suicide is portrayed in everything from TV shows and movies to how it's reported in the news media. I wondered if we had always treaded so gently around the people who take their own lives.

There isn't a lot of historical research analyzing coverage of suicide in the news. Gemma Richardson, a professor of journalism and media at Humber College in Toronto, Canada, is one of the few people who has researched at length how the news media has covered suicides.[1] In Ms. Richardson's studies, she found that the details featured in stories about suicide in newspapers in the nineteenth and twentieth centuries would feel shocking to us today, even in a day of reality TV and nonstop sharing on social media. "Suicide deaths were treated as everyday occurrences and received small mentions along with other local, national and international information," she wrote. She said we only need to look at one item on page two in *The Toronto Globe* on September 4, 1847, to understand how coverage differed: "A carpenter, named Nimbs, committed suicide in Niagara, on the 28th ultimo, by swallowing 55 grains of opium." The news item was followed immediately by a blurb about the monthly meeting of the Toronto Building Society to be held the following Monday. Parts of the newspaper in those days often presented events in chronological order, could seem a mix of a police blotter and calendar. Suicides were reported in the same matter-of-fact style as other information was shared, no matter if the person who died was well known or not, whether they died in a public place or at home. It was reported as news.

By the mid-1850s, Ms. Richardson noted, the reporting of suicides changed from simple facts and details to something that carried more judgment. Suicide at that time often was described as a "rash act," she wrote. Reporters often tried to find a reason for the death and when family or neighbors didn't provide enough detail, the story often said a cause was yet to be determined, as if there was a specific event or action that caused the suicide, and it would soon be definitively discovered.

Coverage of suicide continued evolving, following the path of the news media coverage, and becoming more sensationalized. Later, mentions of suicide mostly disappeared from newspapers. If you only read the newspapers, you would think people died by car accidents and shootings, plane crashes and fires, but only a few famous people killed themselves.

The importance of this study, Ms. Richardson wrote, was that it showed that as public perceptions of suicide, and the laws surrounding it, gradually shifted from considering the act a crime to considering it an aspect of a psychiatric malady, reporting on suicide changed. Once suicide became an untouchable subject in newsrooms, the stigma became entrenched, making it hard to address in any meaningful way for decades.

By the early 1990s, psychologists and others began to look at the correlation between the media reporting on suicides and the contagion factor. Many journalists simply stopped writing about suicide. But researchers, who were seeing the numbers of suicides increase, wanted to learn if the media could help them report on suicide and perhaps help people in the process. In 1994, the Suicide Prevention Resource Center, a group that provides training to increase the knowledge and expertise of professionals serving people at risk of suicide, recommended reporting practices that might reduce the possibility of media-related suicide contagion.[2] They recommended that the media shouldn't describe the technical method used in suicides, meaning that reporting that someone died from carbon monoxide poisoning was OK, but detailing the method was not. They didn't want the media to glorify the person who died, or present it as a means to an end, such as ending depression or pain. The Centers for Disease Control recommended against placing any story about suicide in a prominent place such as the front page, and encouraged media outlets to include any information about suicide hotlines and where to get help.

The difficulty with the guidelines was that they conflicted with much of how journalists approached news. Journalists wanted more details, not fewer—they wanted to showcase a story if it was important and newsworthy. As a reporter and editor, I know that what actually happened was that many in the news media shied away from writing about suicide, preferring not to upset families or violate the new ethical guidelines. So it remained a mostly taboo topic and suicide wasn't covered often.

Not writing about suicide meant that a critical health issue was missing from news coverage. It meant there was little to help encourage a national conversation about suicide and the role mental illness plays. So on the rare occasion when the media did cover suicide, it affected how people perceived it. It shaped how people think about suicide, how they understand it, and even the language we use to talk about it.

I thought back to the story written about my mom when she died at the canyon, the headline that read WOMAN WHO DIED AT CANYON ID'D. It didn't say "suicide," though it did mention in the story that there was a report of a woman who was suicidal. It did mention the last area at the canyon where my mom was seen. When I read the story, I was upset that while the story didn't explicitly say she killed herself, it pointed in that direction. It made me wonder how many people killed themselves that same day in the Phoenix area that we didn't know about because they did so privately. At the time, I was upset that they ran my mom's name. I had yet to really grasp the full understanding of her death, six days afterward, yet here was her death in the newspaper. Even though I was a journalist and had included the names of victims from shootings or other crimes, names of people whose families hadn't approved, I was angry.

That same year my mom died, in 2012, talking about suicide and how to cover it became more common among the news media. Groups such as the American Foundation for Suicide Prevention and others became more active in urging the media to cover suicides sensitively.[3]

In many ways, some of the most important work that Dan Reidenberg has done around suicide has to do with how the media portrays it. Mr. Reidenberg, the executive director of Suicide Awareness Voices of Education, has spent more than two decades trying to help people, particularly the news media and more recently the entertainment industry, talk about suicide with sensitivity and understanding. His group works to prevent suicide through public awareness and education, reducing the stigma, and to serve as a resource to those who have lost someone to suicide.

I met Mr. Reidenberg a few years ago when he asked if I'd like to get involved with his organization and come to its annual remembrance event. He picked me up from the airport in Minneapolis and we talked about how difficult it is for journalists to write or share stories about suicide. They're afraid of writing the wrong thing, I told him, afraid of causing more harm than good. Mr. Reidenberg nodded along, saying he understood. So much has been studied and written about the contagion effect when the media covers suicides that it's no longer disputed.

"We know that how the media portrays suicide can greatly impact the lives of others," he said. Mr. Reidenberg is often called to talk on national morning TV news programs when new studies are released about suicide rates and consulted for movie scripts or books. He understands the importance of his role as a suicide prevention advocate, as well as the role played by the media, and that although the roles differ, they can help each other.

Mr. Reidenberg's organization has helped advocate for responsible reporting since 2011.[4] He is encouraged that he hears from reporters more often now. They sometimes call simply to discuss a story, to ask if their news organization should cover a particular suicide. "That's really a positive thing," he said. "Many media are trying to follow the recommendations, trying to make stories not as sensational, looking at the placement, the language they use, trying to present a more balanced perspective."

The one consistent change he has seen over the years is that most news media now include a number or place where people can seek help, whether it's a national hotline or local resources.

During the drive, I asked him about the idea that our society has now talked more about suicide, but the rates continue to climb. Does it make sense? Does talking about it reduce the stigma, or does it possibly serve as information for copycats? He explained that the simple act of talking about suicide doesn't necessarily destigmatize it. "It's *how* you talk about it," he said. He understands how important and influential the media can be on society's perception and understanding of suicide. He notes that while suicide is discussed more now than at any time in history, the numbers are high.

He cautions that the media cannot simply write about suicide when someone kills themselves. That's the obvious, often sensational way to report. But there are other stories that show how suicide is a public health issue. The media can talk about public health issues in a factual and clear manner—about treatment and support systems, access to care, wait times for treatment centers—and thereby address the issue.

One new theory, he said, looks at the Papageno effect, a term used for stating that there are potentially protective effects of positive messaging, especially in relation to those who have survived suicidal ideation. It correlates positively in the way the Werther effect—the contagion theory—is negative.[5]

"We try to get out a message of hope and recovery," he said of people who have survived a suicide attempt or recovered from deep depression. "If your report on it shows hope and recovery, you can actually reduce the risk of suicide. You don't just have to do a story about someone who died by suicide, but someone who has survived an attempt, and lived a successful life. These are the kinds of stories that can not only change the conversation but reduce the risk others might feel from seeing that story.

"Remember this, Laura," he said. "When journalists can talk about getting help, recovery, going on and living a productive life after treatment, even after an attempt, we can change the entire conversation about suicide and mental health. It can become a story about hope. Yours can be a story of hope."

Chapter 6

Finding Hope

DURING THESE MONTHS, I looked for these moments of optimism and gratitude, and with it came a growing confidence in myself.

As I began to read more about suicide, I found another way to think and talk about it. I learned about the language around it, that when discussing how someone died, it's important to use the right words, and that in fact saying "commit" is wrong. Psychologists and those who study suicide suggest that the acceptable way to say it is "died by suicide," or "killed herself," because the word *commit* conveys a feeling of crime or wrongdoing, which perhaps we don't want to give.

I wish there was a phrase like there is in Spanish. I remember in my high school Spanish class, I learned a phrase, *el vaso se rompio*. There is no blame—"the vase broke itself." I wondered if there was a way to say, she broke, my mom broke herself. And she did, *mi mama se rompio*. Or another phrase that my friend's father used to use when a lightbulb burnt out: *la luz se fue*. It translates literally to "the light left," which felt like what happened with my mom.

I knew I would then begin to change the way I talked about my mom. The shift in my language and description reflected a shift within myself. My mom did kill herself. She didn't commit suicide. She was not a victim. I was not a survivor. She died by suicide, and I was starting to be OK with saying it, though not necessarily talking about it, two very different things. During the months before this shift in both how I talked about suicide or even thought about it, several things happened to help me find the gratitude in my own life.

John had had juvenile diabetes since he was a teenager. It had been thirty-five years of low and high blood sugar levels, and it began to put a strain on his arteries and heart, his kidneys and nerves. We decided that John should have a pancreas transplant to deal with his diabetes. He had always been good at controlling his blood sugar, so good that when I met him, we dated for months before I knew he was diabetic. We had managed his disease for years, him, mostly, but with me helping. Later he'd been able to use an insulin pump, a device the size of a pager. Instead of insulin injections through a syringe, he could tell the pump to deliver insulin. It helped him regulate his sugar much better, constantly delivering a drip, and then allowing him to push insulin to his body without shots.

Just before we moved to Cincinnati, his blood sugar was dropping or rising seemingly at random, no longer following a pattern, and his body no longer reacted to insulin in the same way. The pump no longer was working. It worried him, and I worried that the damage from the stress on his organs from the high or low sugars might cause a heart attack or stroke, or dangerous lows that would be difficult to catch. It made me afraid to have him drive.

About nine months after we had moved to Cincinnati and six months after my mom died, John's doctor recommended a pancreas transplant, a rare surgery that works for diabetics who are sick enough to qualify for the organ, but healthy enough to survive the surgery and ongoing transplant protocol. We figured it was his best shot.

John was added to the transplant list at one of our large hospitals in Cincinnati. He would need to be reachable by the hospital and available at any time. We knew the surgery would be intense, as would his recovery. He needed to know that I was ready to take care of the children, and him, to be the caregiver if he received a transplant.

The call came on All Saints' Day in 2013. The transplant went well; the recovery did not. The next five months after surgery are a blur.

Yet the pancreas transplant ultimately not only saved John but also helped to save me. I didn't realize it at the time, but it gave me a renewed purpose. I felt more needed, to take care of him after he had taken care of me. I wanted the future we could look forward to.

By that spring, John was healthy, and I was sick of listening to myself in therapy sessions. Work was busy, the kids seemed good, I felt mostly like I could breathe again. We celebrated our health with a family trip. At some point early that year in 2014, I threw out the goodbye notes I had written to my children and replaced them with something else, a checklist of sorts. It was a list of questions, something to review when things didn't feel right. The list is below. I felt that if I knew enough to look at the list, I would be OK. The trouble would be if I didn't know enough to look at the list. I felt I had help enough that would lead me to the list. So I felt I would be OK. As I look at the list now, I see it has a lot to do with confronting problems, and thinking about others, how to help others.

Take your medicine, even if you think you don't need to. (You will think you don't need to at some point, but that means the medicine is working, which means, of course, that you need it.)

Talk to someone. Are you doing that?

Compliment someone today. You likely are thinking something nice in your head, so say it out loud. It always makes someone smile, which will make you feel better. The other person, too.

Go outside. Put your feet on the actual earth.

Do something useful for someone else, without being asked. Make coffee for someone else. Make the kids' lunches. Fold laundry. Offer to help someone at work.

Write something and share it. Doesn't have to be about Mom, just something to be part of the world. Just post something on Facebook. If someone comments, comment back.

Do you still feel bad? Don't be alone for the next day, see how you feel. Ask someone to do something. Go for a walk, to lunch or coffee, something.

Still bad? But you knew to look at this list, so you are OK. Do these things. Promise. (Read me again in a week, and you'll know.) If you don't feel better, call your therapist.

The note is still here. I don't look for it anymore, but I know that I will keep it, not because I need it, but because I need to see where I used to be so that I can see where I am now. Now and then when I am putting away laundry, I unfold it and re-read the words, remembering the times when I needed to see them. I remind myself that I never want to be there again. Sometimes I make sure I do some of the things on the list without looking at the note.

It doesn't mean things became perfect, because they weren't, and rarely ever are, but incrementally things started to improve. I wish I could say that it was because I had four sweet children and a dear husband, daily reminders that I couldn't continue to be satisfied with sliding through what my life had become, getting by and wishing I wouldn't wake up each morning, reminders that I was OK. But my mind didn't quite let me see that. My mind would at times tell me, "They'll be better off without you." In time, things happened that made me see they needed me.

Gradually, I started to realize I was hiding what happened to my mom—see, I'm using the word *happened*—rather than saying what she did as a more passive way of discussing it. Was I trying to protect her or me? Or both of us? Did it matter? In the beginning I felt not telling helped me. If I didn't say what she did, it didn't mean it didn't happen (I still had logic), but it meant I didn't have to deal with it. And dealing with it, the suicide, meant dealing with the guilt I felt—that in the very best scenario I didn't do enough, and in the worst, I was responsible.

But I knew that it now was important to me to say how she died, not to avoid it. I wasn't sure exactly why. Was not talking about my mom's suicide and not knowing exactly what happened making me too comfortable? I wanted to learn how to talk about it, how to say it.

After I started reading more about suicide, I learned how to talk about it, how to describe it, and as important, how *not* to describe it. I didn't like it when people referred to themselves as a victim of suicide when they had lost someone, nor did I like saying that I was a survivor of suicide, because it requires the brain to think too much to figure it out. And the words are wrong: I didn't survive suicide— I hadn't tried to kill myself.

So at some point, when someone asked what happened to my mom, I told the truth. I said she committed suicide. I wanted to be able to tell the truth and share the story, and it felt as if it would protect those who died, and it also protected me. It felt safe, a way to say she died without saying "death." It softened her death. I thought it was the right thing to say, the way the phrase sounded: simple, less violent and jarring. *Commit* felt like a good word—people commit themselves to marriage or improving their tennis game, they commit to going meatless, or running a marathon by the age of forty. I decided to ignore the fact that people also use the word when they say someone commits murder or a crime. *Commit* had a good connotation to me at this time, before I knew more. The word *suicide* on its own takes on its own meaning. People begin to fill in the familiar, going to a place they know—suicide in history, Sylvia Plath, or Ernest Hemingway. Depending on their age or stage of life, they go to Kurt Cobain or Robin Williams, Kate Spade or Anthony Bourdain. Their mind moves away from what we're talking about, and this was exactly what I wanted. Suicide becomes less about the person who's gone, and more about the unknowable, the deep mystery of it.

When you tell someone you lost someone to suicide, there generally are two reactions. Some quietly distance themselves from the conversation that maybe is too confounding, too close, too something so that we don't even want to discuss it. Maybe it's that it feels too awful, too scary. Maybe you, too, have thought about it. Because the reality is that many people have thought about it, which is a much bigger number than those who have tried it, still a bigger number than those who have actually done it. But it puts you closer to that subset that feels like you want to be further away from. So there's an "Oh," sometimes not even an "I'm sorry," just a way of trying to get out of the conversation as quickly as you can.

For others, you mention suicide, and you get a knowing look, and usually a story, sometimes you are prepared for, and sometimes you are not. There is someone else who knows, a comfort in some weird way reminding you that you aren't the only one who has felt this, who has gone through this, who right there is standing up and talking and participating in the world, and maybe you are further ahead of them, or behind, but here they are, alive, and how is that? But you know if they are, there might also be a way that you can, too, stand here, that is, and maybe discuss it, or maybe not, and to not worry that bringing it up feels like you have passed a statute of limitations or something on discussing. It's not quite grief, though that is there—it's a gnawing, a sadness, and sometimes guilt. And you don't understand the gift of telling your story, until you do. The pain could have a purpose.

Chapter 7

Getting Better

EVERY YEAR ON the anniversary of my mom's death, I wanted to visit the place where she died. At first I thought I wanted to go be with her, to end my life the way she did. Later, as I got better, I realized I wanted to go to the canyon to learn more, to see what she saw, to feel what she might have felt that morning. I studied the photo she took at the ledge on her last day, zooming in to see if something would show me something, anything to bring me closer to her. The more I zoomed, the blurrier it became, and the less I knew. By the fourth anniversary of her death, I felt I was finally ready, if there could be such a thing as ready.

I had requested the report from the National Park Service, which oversees the Grand Canyon. While I waited for the report, I called the ranger's office to see if they could help me find the spot where my mother died.

Ranger Shannon Miller agreed to meet me at the canyon.

"Will you be alone?" she asked me.

"No."

"Good," she said.

I had asked my best friend from Phoenix, Sara, if she might go with me to the canyon. I could fly to Phoenix and we could drive to the canyon together. I've known Sara for almost as long as I've been a mom, meeting her when my eldest child and her second eldest child started preschool together. She'd lived around the corner from me in central Phoenix and we used to run together in the early mornings before the sun would rise and the temperatures would hit a hundred degrees. We bonded as working moms who loved words, me as a journalist and she as the president of a public relations company. As we ran, we talked about our children, our jobs, our failings, and our worries. Sara knew as much about me as I had let anyone know.

I asked if she was certain she wanted to come with me. "I might cry a lot," I warned. "It's not going to be super fun. But I want you there. I think I need it."

She laughed.

"Laura, you asked me to come to the spot where your mom killed herself. I don't think it's going to be, you know, a fun girls' road trip."

She reminded me that she had been present for someone giving birth as well as someone dying, and that everything would be OK. I had to promise not to jump. Sara offered to put me on a harness and child leash to keep me safe.

She also knew how to make me laugh.

I flew in to Phoenix and Sara picked me up at the airport.

Even as I was getting better, there remained a yawning uncertainty about my mom, and questions, so many questions. I felt like the only way I could be fully better, to not feel eternally haunted by her death, was to understand her and her death better.

Twelve other people had died at the Grand Canyon the year my mother died—falls, heart attacks, and suicides, mostly. Enough people die at our fifty-eight national parks that the National Park Service has created a special team at each park to help deal with death. They are there to investigate and understand, to find the next of kin to provide information and some context where there might not seem to be any, and sometimes, simply to stand quietly next to you.

My mom first saw the Grand Canyon as an adult, a visit with her sister shortly after she and my dad divorced. Later she hiked rim to rim with her sister, 23.5 miles from the North Rim and back up the South Rim, a hike that's revered in Arizona, a point of pride—the equivalent of a 26.2 oval marathon sticker on the back of your car. She hiked the canyon the last time maybe a decade before she died, taking an easy trail with her husband, whose knees and hips, which had endured years of competitive skiing, had begun to bother him.

Sara and I drove to the canyon from Phoenix as an April storm moved in and the sky darkened. It's just over a three-hour drive, a straight shot north on the I-17 through the Sonoran Desert and then the Coconino and Kaibab National Forests. I realized my mom would have made this drive in the middle of the night or maybe just before dawn.

As we gained altitude, the tall saguaros gave way to scrubby bushes and later to ponderosa pine trees at sixty-nine hundred feet. We passed the spot where six hundred years ago the Sinagua people lived high in the limestone cliffs of Montezuma Castle, and where the settlers traveled through heat to be the first to mine for salt at Camp Verde. Mule deer and elk dotted the roadside. By the time we reached Flagstaff in northern Arizona, about ninety minutes from the canyon, it was snowing and the temperature had dropped more than fifty-five degrees.

It is a long time, Mom, I thought, to change your mind.

Sara and I drove the next hour and a half, mostly not saying much, but not being uncomfortable about it either. It was good to have a friend like that, a great gift. We checked in to a room at the Bright Angel Lodge with a window overlooking the South Rim of the canyon. She reminded me that however things unfolded today, we had dinner reservations at El Tovar, an elegant, yet casual enough restaurant for you to wear your hiking boots, which somehow still feels natural among the rustic and sparse buildings around the canyon. It's a place where President Theodore Roosevelt had dinner, as did Paul McCartney, and where you can get a duck tamale or a $210 bottle of cabernet sauvignon. It's known for food as incredible as the views.

"We also have wine," she said, reminding me that we bought that pinot noir at Walgreens when we stopped in Flagstaff.

We hadn't anticipated the severe temperature drop when we left Phoenix, and I forgot to check the weather, so we each layered on thin cardigans and pullover sweaters to stay warm.

"You'll be all right," she said, hugging me before we left our room.

The ranger and I agreed to meet at Bright Angel Lodge, the main place visitors to the canyon likely will stop, and the first place built for visitors at the national park. It's a gorgeous old cabin built in 1935 out of old timber and stone, carefully crafted to preserve the native trees, shrubs, and flowers that surround it. Toward the rim or the top of the canyon, the Bright Angel Trail is good for tourists who want to take day hikes, those wearing flip-flops or dress shoes, or those who simply want to stop for a short walk and maybe a selfie. It's a trail with shade and water for those who might want to take a day hike to the popular Indian Gardens stop four and a half miles down. It's a trail that slowly winds its way up with water stops, and is easy for first-time hikers to take into or out of the canyon.

Bright Angel Lodge is where you can pick up a permit to camp at the canyon's floor, check in to one of the sparse rooms where families gather and hikers use as a base camp, or reserve a mule that will carry you into the canyon as well as out while also carrying a bag of garbage from the bottom of the canyon at Phantom Ranch. It's where you can stop in the gift shop to buy an "I Hiked the Canyon" T-shirt, a toddler-sized ranger replica uniform, a dream catcher made by Native Americans for $26 or one made in China for $1.99, a panoramic postcard pack, and a bottle of water with a picture of the canyon on it. It's where I bought a hoodie that says "Grand Canyon National Park" across it.

There was a wall of books in the store, several about Fred Harvey and the Harvey Girls, whose existence was part of why I was there. Mr. Harvey came from England as a teenager and after the Civil War, he followed the railroad west. He didn't think any restaurants were good enough along the way, and decided to build his own. Each one had to have the same high quality as the last, down to the "girls" who worked at the restaurant counters. The women who worked there became known as Harvey Girls. Mr. Harvey worked his way west along the rails, even convincing railroad executives to extend the line up to the canyon, which had recently opened as a tourist spot. He saw the canyon as a way to make money. He continued all the way to California, with more than one hundred Harvey Houses in all. To this day, Mr. Harvey remains legendary in the hospitality industry, known as one of the first to standardize quality service.

Among the other books, mostly guides to hiking trails, river rafting, and the geology of the canyon, I found something: *Over the Edge: Death in Grand Canyon: Gripping Accounts of All Known Fatal Mishaps in the Most Famous of the World's Seven Natural Wonders*. It boasted, "Newly expanded 10th anniversary edition." A placard with a Christmas ornament on it read, "Gift Idea!" It's the work of Michael P. Ghiglieri and Thomas M. Myers, who said in the book's introduction that they wanted to share incredible tales of survival and rescues as well as tragedies of more than 750 people who have died at the canyon.[1]

I picked it up, glancing around to see if anyone was watching. There was a story of John Wesley Powell, the first to explore the Colorado River that cut through the canyon, and that of the TWA and United airplanes that collided over the rim in 1956 killing all 128 people aboard, and led to the creation of the Federal Aviation Administration. There were stories of survival, hikers who got lost and told harrowing tales of making it to safety, and sad stories of tourists not paying attention or goofing off and falling to their deaths in the canyon.

I flipped through to chapter 9, "Suicide." On page 470, I found her. My mom.

"April 26, 2012. Trailview Overlook

Jumped off the rim. 100 feet. Grand Canyon News Release, May 2, 2012."

I felt sick. How could she be in this book? I hadn't told them they could use her name. She was just one paragraph in between a forty-seven-year-old man who had jumped five hundred feet to his death ten days before my mother died and a thirty-six-year-old man who'd driven his car off the South Rim in 2013, ejected 425 feet down, and died later that day. Overall, the book seemed to be well researched, including interviews with rangers and hikers, and it was written by an author who serves as medical advisor for the park and knows it well, and another man who volunteers for the Coconino County Sheriff's Search and Rescue team. It traces the first known suicide at the canyon back to 1914 when a Civil War Purple Heart veteran killed himself below the South Rim, likely with a pistol, the book said.

But parts of the chapter on suicide provided an outdated understanding, one that I still hear today. The book called suicide a selfish act. The authors wrote, "Sadly, what most people who commit a spectacular suicide fail to understand in their self-absorption is: No one is dazzled by their actions. Pity is the very most they ever get." Though the authors do concede, "We oppose the tragic aftermath of suicide, the devastating psychological mess and legacy of horror that suicides leave. Again, it eternally haunts the parents, siblings, spouses, and/or children of the victim. Suicide lingers as a miasmic evil for generations."

The book barely mentioned my mom. But I bit my bottom lip to keep from crying. My mom's story wasn't theirs to tell. I put the book down.

Sara and I left the gift shop and walked to the lodge and waited for the ranger. Sara stood back a few feet. I had told the ranger I would meet her on the front wood steps, knowing I would recognize her in her uniform. I had tried to explain what I looked like, but then started to tell her how nervous and anxious I would look, describing what my face would look like with all of the feelings it would be holding inside without actually telling her what I would be wearing or what I looked like. "Maybe it will be easier if you just find me," she had suggested.

I saw a woman in a uniform and introduced myself.

"Ready?" Ms. Miller asked me. She had that just-right mix of ranger and detective, and her smile felt like a hug.

She told me to hop in to my car and follow her Forest Service pickup truck through a special gate that allows only shuttle buses and authorized park service trucks. I felt guilty at first, my friend's white sedan snaking past the gate into the unauthorized zone, like I was allowed past the velvet rope or VIP area, or somewhere I didn't belong. Then I laughed nervously, realizing how absurd an idea that seemed—we weren't getting special access at a Las Vegas club. We drove along the Rim Trail, which winds anywhere from twenty to forty feet from the edge of the canyon, to the Trailview Overlook, the first stop for the canyon's shuttle bus route following the Rim Trail. It was less than two miles from the lodge where we had just met.

We parked and met next to the ranger's truck.

Ms. Miller and her husband both worked at the canyon,

where they'd lived the past several years and raised their young son.

Sara found a quiet spot to wait.

Ms. Miller and I walked down a concrete path along the canyon, juniper trees on the left, a ledge and waist-high metal pipe handrail on the right, the same path my mom would have taken. I could see a short fence and jagged limestone that formed an overlook. When we neared the spot, Ms. Miller pulled yellow caution tape from her bag and cordoned off the trail.

"You might want some quiet," she said. "Some privacy."

I looked around, worried that this small barricade was an intrusion and could ruin someone's view on their only trip to the canyon. I saw a woman walk toward the overlook, reach the tape, and turn around. I mouthed, "I'm sorry."

The ranger smiled, and laughed a little, pointing out to the canyon. "There are many places to see the canyon, Laura, no shortages here. She'll be able to see," she said. "For now, this is your spot. It's better this way."

The area is unremarkable, of course, with an amazing view. This location is known for having one of the best views from the South Rim. There's the canyon, looking more three-dimensional than the photos you've seen, and greener because you can actually see the trees. But there also are the San Francisco Peaks, a gorgeous range of volcanic mountains sixty-five miles in the distance. You don't know where to look. The colors of the canyon change as you look deeper, from a deep rust to an almost white, and then spots that look almost purple from shadows.

Sara stood back about fifteen feet on a large flat piece of white rock with tan veins jutting up over the canyon, where she sat down and pulled the arms of her sweater to cover her hands.

The ranger and I talked about everything but my mom at first. I looked down at my sandals and asked her about the rock where we stood. First she pointed out the piñon bushes and Utah juniper, which thrive at this elevation, the highest point, and told me that under our feet was limestone, the Kaibab layer and one of eight layers of the canyon. It's 270 million years old, the youngest layer of the canyon, an area that once was covered with warm, shallow, and clear seawater on top of a muddy or sandy bar. Its name is Paiute Indian and means "mountain lying down," and somehow I like that image. It makes no sense and yet is perfect. It's where you would have found clams and snails.

Each layer of the canyon is formed by the Colorado River. The rock at the bottom, the Vishnu Schist, is two billion years old, half as old as the earth. Ms. Miller talked volcanos and rivers, snow and dry wind, tectonic plates and tributaries widening the canyon, about how Native people roamed this area for thousands of years before tribal groups began to settle more than one thousand years ago.

I listened, in part, hearing words I remembered from Arizona history class in a Phoenix classroom as a ninth grader, and taking in new information. Her running geological description was soothing, a meditation of sorts that felt maybe the way those plug-in water fountains are supposed to feel. My eyes wandered to the edge, as did my head, imagining my mom that morning.

I took a step closer as we talked, and another, and realized I was walking to the ledge.

Up until 1858, the area was still known as the Great Unknown, when John Newberry was the first scientist to reach the canyon floor. As both a physician and geologist, he recognized the canyon's significance in the study of the earth, but he also understood its beauty. Even with as much as we know, there's still some debate as to how the canyon formed and the Colorado River's relatively new role in it. The simple reason that it's so difficult to know isn't that it took millions of years to create and we're trying to understand it in one lifetime, but that the canyon has mostly been shaped by erosion, and that means most of the evidence has been washed away. The canyon's sheer size—stretching 277 miles from one end to the next—shows that all of the canyon wasn't even formed at the same time. Geologists have suggested that the canyon is between seventy million and six million years old, depending on the area, Ms. Miller said.

The simplest explanation of the canyon, she said, is that the Colorado River carved it, and that forces on the walls, running water from rain and snowmelt, continue to widen the canyon today. The erosion creates slopes in places, sheer drops in others—the vivid colors of red, yellow, and green, which can look purple in the light, are the result of minerals. The canyon formation also involves the ocean withdrawing from the area eighty million years ago, leaving a lowland where rivers formed, tectonic plates lifted, and four remarkable plateaus emerged. The rocks in the canyon walls show the Paleozoic Era (541 to 252 million years ago) and at the bottom, there are Precambrian rocks, two billion years old. But really, she said, the origin of the canyon remains mostly elusive to geologists. They have theories and are getting closer to better understanding it—but unlike the origin of Yosemite, Yellowstone, and other parks, there remains some mystery about this canyon.

We walked closer toward the canyon, inching closer to the ledge, as close as we could, while staying behind the chain-link fence that separated us from the edge. I set my right hand on the cold metal bar at the top of the rail. I craned my neck over, somehow losing my fear of heights in a moment of morbid curiosity and complete loss of awareness about where I was.

I peered over, looking down, farther now, to a ledge about one hundred feet below, where I saw scrubby brown earth, pebbles, and openness, with a few pine trees and a piñon. It looked like a shelf jutting out on the way to the bottom.

"There?" I asked.

"Yes, there," Ms. Miller said.

"It looks different," I said. Just one hundred feet down, the terrain had already changed, with dirt a different color and texture, and plants that wouldn't survive where we stood. That ledge was where my mom had landed.

"It's the Coconino layer," Ms. Miller explained, a layer that formed 275 million years ago. The light sandstone formed a broad cliff. The lines in this layer, the cross-bedding that run through it, reveal the story of an area that used to be covered with dunes, the wind blowing them into shapes, over and over again. It appears there are waves within the rocks.

I got lost in the geology for a moment, standing in a place that held rocks two billion years old, and my brain placed the two and six . . . no, *nine* zeroes to the right. That's not forever but an amount of time I could not comprehend.

I focused on the facts. The trees and rocks, how the Colorado River snaked below almost exactly one mile down into the earth, the sound of a raven and the light rain that was slowly growing heavier and turning to snow.

My mom fell five million years.

"It's cold."

That's all I could say.

Ms. Jean Drevecky drove the Paul Revere shuttle bus on the Hermits Rest and Village route that fourth Thursday morning of April 2012. The bus, which runs on natural gas, transports passengers from the visitor center along seven miles of the canyon. During the canyon's busy season, which begins in March, people sometimes wait at shuttle stops for two or three buses before there's room to hop on. It's also the time of year that private cars aren't allowed to drive along the canyon, so the shuttle is the only way to get to some of the more popular overlooks or hiking trails. The shuttle bus stops in nine places with lookout points, hiking trails, and a gift shop and place for snacks. The bus itself is less a tourist destination—there rarely are good views from it as the canyon is often separated from the road by pine trees and trails. It's a practical and free way to get to hiking trails without actually hiking to reach them.

On Ms. Drevecky's first shuttle bus round that morning at 6:45, she picked up a woman at the stop closest to the visitor center. That woman was my mom. Ms. Drevecky remembered that the woman sat alone, quiet, her hands in her coat pockets "like perhaps she was cold." The woman seemed calm and had approached Ms. Drevecky, asking where she could take photos of "steep canyon walls." They discussed the views at Trailview Overlook, Maricopa Point, and Powell Point, the first three stops on the loop, each of which offer amazing views and places to stop to take photographs. The woman took a seat and then got off the bus five minutes later at the first stop the shuttle made that morning, at Trailview Overlook. Later the shuttle bus driver would say she didn't remember seeing the woman carrying a backpack or camera.

Phone records show that my mom called her husband four times that morning, beginning at 2:15 A.M., then 5:05 A.M., neither of which were answered. At 6:34 A.M., she reached him, and told him she was at the Grand Canyon. The last call she made to him was at 6:56 A.M., when she began to cry and told him she was at the canyon's first shuttle bus stop.

He told rangers that she was crying, saying, "This is it. I am finished. I cannot go on." He said he tried to talk to her about the good things in her life. The ranger report doesn't detail what he meant by that, but together my mom and her husband had scuba dived in the Great Barrier Reef, flown in a hot-air balloon above Albuquerque, skied the Alps in France and Switzerland, and driven their motor home to Alaska. He'd taught her how to water-ski and sail a catamaran, fly-fish, and kayak. He'd found the adventurer in my mom. But in the end, the secrets that emerged broke her, too. They broke all of us.

On the phone, she did not say goodbye.

Her husband said to the rangers that he felt like he was in a state of shock. The call lasted four minutes.

"Your mom must have known this place pretty well," Ms. Miller said, noting that of all the miles of canyons here, my mom knew the spot to jump where she wouldn't hurt anyone and would be easy to find, and it wouldn't be difficult for rescuers to retrieve her body. I was quiet for a moment, for once not feeling the need to fill the space. I nodded. We spoke in facts, without emotion. It was better that way, I decided. I pretended I was simply a reporter learning the story.

But in fact I am also her daughter, trying to find answers.

"We have people not as courteous as your mom," Ms. Miller told me.

This sentence has stuck with me. My mom was courteous, even then.

She left her Jeep parked in the lot outside of Bright Angel Lodge, suicide notes tucked into her purse inside. She safety pinned the name of her husband and his phone number on to her jacket, whom to call to claim her bruised and broken body, so her family wouldn't need to worry, she could be identified and recovered.

"Yes" was all I could say, thinking about all the ways my mom had been courteous in her life, of how she wrote cards and notes to all her patients recovering from heart attacks, how she still made my dad's father his favorite fudge long after she and my dad were divorced, and would bring it by on Christmas Eve and help her former mother-in-law get ready for a party my mom would no longer attend.

I looked down Bright Angel Trail, my eyes following the twenty-seven switchbacks I counted until they grew too tiny and disappeared into the canyon. I'd been here before, I realized. With her.

Chapter 8

———

Hiking with My Mother

THE SUMMER AFTER my freshman year of college, I came home and my mom said, "Why don't we hike the canyon?"

I knew she loved the place. I'd never hiked it. I'd seen it once when I was young, but only from the rim, an overlook, the same one from which she would later jump, actually.

Hiking the canyon together would be the most time my mom and I had spent together, just the two of us. My mom took a day off from work, and we drove to the Grand Canyon on a Friday morning, sharing a double bed in a hotel overlooking the South Rim that night. The next day we woke before the sun to take a shuttle bus to the trailhead of the South Kaibab Trail, seven steep miles down and known for some of the best panoramic views of the canyon along the hike.

"Better down than up," my mom said in the happy singsong voice she used when my sister and I were kids and faced something difficult, and something I now sometimes hear in my own voice. I try to remember the details of our hike now, but can't—only certain memories of it linger. But do I really remember them or are they only memories built from photos?

It was decades before the Hydro Flask or AirPods. I wore a canteen with a shoulder strap and my white leather Reeboks. I had brought a Walkman with black foam headphones, the cord clumsily leading to my backpack. I brought just one tape, Depeche Mode's *Some Great Reward,* the tape I remember arguing with my sister about in the driveway before we left, insisting it was mine and I could take it on the trip. It was 1989 and I would not own a CD player for another three years.

We carried water and a log of sliced salami, string cheese, and a peach. I still remember we didn't eat the peach, and the bumpy hike down turned the fruit to mush in my JanSport backpack that would still smell of peaches when I returned to school. This trail had no shade and no stops for water, so we knew we wanted to reach the bottom well before noon.

The start of the hike was an endless descent of tight, steep switchbacks through the limestone layers of the canyon. We rode the shuttle bus to the trailhead with more than a dozen people, and when we started the hike, groups hiked in front of us and behind, but partway in, groups found their own pace, leaving my mom and me to feel as if we had the canyon to ourselves. We reached a point near Cedar Ridge where the trail mercifully leveled off, and it felt like an easy afternoon hike through a scrubby, dry, flat desert for a good while and where your body feels like it is just walking, not bracing itself with each step. Then the sharp descent returned. We crossed the Kaibab Suspension Bridge over the Colorado

River, jumping in the middle of the bridge like children to see how much we could make it shake. After four and a half hours of hiking, we reached the canyon's floor, a severe drop in elevation to 2,570 feet. The temperature that early September day hit 101 degrees. Near the Colorado River, it was as humid as a sauna.

After we crossed the muddy-looking Colorado, among the cottonwood trees we spotted Phantom Ranch, the only lodging at the canyon's floor. When you first see it, you think it must be a mirage. How would there be a hotel at the bottom of the canyon? Just along the Bright Angel Creek, the land was once used by Native Americans, and a kiva—a ceremonial room the Pueblo Indians used—dating back to the year 1050 was found there. President Theodore Roosevelt stayed at the camp area, which later was seen as a spot to build a hotel, except for one problem: All materials to build the hotel would need to be brought from the top of the canyon by mule. The lodge and its nearby cabins were designed by Mary Elizabeth Jane Colter, one of the most important architects at the canyon. In a time when there were very few women architects, she was a perfectionist, who designed around the canyon one building at a time. She pioneered a design aesthetic to blend in to its surroundings to give them a sense of place. It became a style that is reflected in many of the buildings at our national parks as well as in buildings across the country. Phantom Ranch was made with native stones and wood hauled down miles of trails. It can only be reached by hiking to the bottom of the canyon, by raft, or by mule.

The ranch has a dining hall in the lodge for meals, a few cabins set up like dormitories, private cabins, and a campground. My mom and I chose the easy hiker's choice, opting for a room in the dorm, and dinner cooked at the lodge, and fresh water to fill our canteens. This way we wouldn't need to carry a tent, sleeping bags, or any more food than our snacks, making our backpacks much lighter and the hike easier. Phantom Ranch is where trails from the South Rim and less popular North Rim join, where river rafters often stop, where the mules rest for the night before carrying out trash from Phantom Ranch, and where postcards are stamped MAILED BY MULE before they are carried to the rim. It also is a place where a helipad—there for rescues—reminds you of the dangers of the canyon.

At the bottom of the canyon we dropped our packs and hiked to Bright Angel Creek, a clear creek that makes its way down the north side of the canyon and drains into the Colorado River. We took our shoes and socks off, and dipped our feet in the water, sitting on red rocks near the edge, and not saying a thing, not needing to, just trying to take it all in. The sun was intense and the trees turn to scrubby bushes in this spot, yet the water was still cold. Being at the bottom of the Grand Canyon feels like being tucked as far inside the earth as you can be, knowing the rocks near you are half as old as the planet itself. Looking up to the reds and purples of the canyon walls, the creek that comes from Roaring Springs, and the blue cloudless sky, you feel as if you are in your own world. Less than 1 percent of the five million people who visit the Grand Canyon each year make it to the bottom. And briefly, as you stand there among the sounds of the creek and river, it makes you think you have a tiny idea of what it felt like to be an astronaut and look down to earth, but we were looking away from earth.

After a while, we both worried about ever having to stand up again or put back on our shoes, reminding ourselves we had a hike out the next day.

My mom and I shared a cabin with eight other women. The cabin was lined with bunk beds, and my mom offered me the bottom bunk, knowing I wouldn't sleep well up on the top one. I had insisted on the vegetarian option for dinner, declaring that year as a college freshman that I no longer ate meat, so my mom and I ate vegetable stew and corn bread. We shared a giant piece of chocolate cake with fudge frosting and proclaimed it the best dinner we'd ever had, knowing it was partially that we were really hungry from the hike. We would talk and laugh about that cake for years: It became the cake by which all other desserts were measured.

Later that night, we sat with other hikers on halved logs forming a U shape under the cottonwood trees, and we looked into the darkest of skies filled with stars. One of the park rangers talked about light pollution and how we were in one of the darkest places in Arizona so that on a clear night, we could see more stars than we might see anywhere else. The ranger pointed out constellations as we traced them in the air with our fingers. Another ranger began a story about Glen and Bessie, newlyweds who had rafted down the Colorado River in 1928 for their honeymoon. If they'd finished the trip, Bessie would have been the first woman to raft the entire river, but the couple disappeared. Their bodies were never recovered and while many presume they were killed in the rapids, rumors and legends took hold, including one that Bessie killed Glen and hiked out alone. I listened as I leaned into my mom, her hair smelling like

Ivory because she washed it with a bar of soap. I fell asleep on her shoulder.

The next morning, we woke before the sun again, skipped breakfast, filled our canteens at a water spigot outside Phantom Ranch lodge, and headed out on the longer, but gentler, Bright Angel Trail to the top. This trail is two miles longer than the one we took to the bottom, but much less steep. From the beginning, it feels different from the South Kaibab Trail. You follow creeks and a river instead of ridge lines. I remember the first mile following the Colorado River, and looking up five thousand feet of canyon walls, and wondering how long it would take us to ever hike out. I don't know what we talked about on that hike, I can't remember how much we spoke. Did I have my headphones on the whole walk? Did Walkman batteries last that long? I remember being so tired on the way up, thinking those last switchbacks would never end, and my mom pushing ahead of me. She was forty-four, younger than I am now, and I was about the age my second eldest son is now.

I try to think of what it was like then, how I viewed her and how much I am like her now. I always thought of her as strong and smart, sensible and confident, like she knew how to be a mom, how to treat a fever and when to worry, when to push us and when to let us find our way. She would let me go by myself to Europe the next summer just after the wall came down in Germany, backpacking from Poland to Spain. I sent her a few postcards and called her once that summer. Now I worry, talking with Henry about college or Theo about his friends, that I don't possess that confidence or bravery to know your kids are OK, that there's some type of guidebook to motherhood I didn't read. Do my kids sense that this is just an experiment I'm feeling my way through? I wish my mom were here to talk to and answer questions.

On the way up, I do remember that my mom told stories about the Grand Canyon, how she had camped at Indian Gardens, a beautiful spot where we filled our canteens. She talked about hiking Hermit Trail, too, the steep one at the end of the Rim Trail. She'd been to Havasupai, a place believed to be sacred, with water so turquoise you don't believe it's real, and she'd camped on the North Rim, a quieter spot with few tourists. She said she had done everything she wanted at the Grand Canyon except raft the Colorado River. It was on her list, she said, someday.

As we walked the never-ending switchbacks up, an older man came from the left in a narrow spot where there isn't a lot of room to pass. It reminded me that while hiking you must yield to mules. The mules, which carry food to the bottom and carry trash out, get the inside wall, and you get the edge. As we walked in sync for a few minutes, my mom, as always, had a happy hello and she chatted with him a bit. He was around seventy, or that's what he looked like to my teenage self. Soon his stride was longer, his walk much faster, and he nodded and passed us. The last mile of the hike felt as if it took forever—with every switchback we were certain it would be the last. When we reached the top, we saw the man who had passed us, standing at a rail taking photos of ravens. He congratulated us, and out of breath, we both strained to say thank you. He took our photo next to the trail sign, and we gave him our address to mail the photo to us when he developed his film.

The photo hung on my bulletin board in my dorm the

next year. My mom is smiling—her red hair is permed into curls and looks blond in spots in the sun. Her arms are straight at her sides, the sleeves of her T-shirt rolled once, her baggy khaki shorts hanging on her thin body, her thick hiking socks rolled down to her sneakers. My dark hair is pulled up in a ponytail. I'm wearing purple shorts with a paper bag waist, a peach T-shirt, thick socks, white Reeboks, and my black Swatch. My canteen is slung over my left shoulder, my headphones resting on my neck. It's hard to tell if I'm happy, or just exhausted. Is her smile real? I'm carrying her larger orange pack with a light metal frame and thick, padded straps with the hiking boots that gave her a blister inside.

Every picture from the past—even this one from twenty years before her death—now gets studied from time to time. Does she look happy? Was she happy? It's possible to be happy and not. It's just one moment from about thirty years ago and I don't have the answer. How does someone go from happy to suicide, or is that really the path? Was she truly happy or did we just miss the clues to her unhappiness? The photo now sits on my desk, next to my laptop, for me to pick up and examine, and wonder.

My mom and I celebrated our hike by eating chocolate ice cream in sugar cones at a stand at Bright Angel Lodge, and then we drove back to Phoenix early that evening. My legs ached every time I had to push the clutch of her stick-shift Nissan sedan on the way home. We both had to work the next day.

Chapter 9

Piecing Together My Mom's Life

THE REPORT CAME from the U.S. Department of the Interior National Park Service. Everyone in my family finally told me what they knew, but no one had put it all together to fully see my mom. She had not told everyone exactly how she was feeling, and maybe she didn't know. Even if we shared, it was only small stories and none of us could see all the pieces after she was gone. She had been dying and we didn't see it.

It didn't look like what we might think people look like when they are dying, or the way we tend to expect people to look, the weakness, the loss of weight, and eventually, the shutting down of organs, of breath. It looked, in retrospect, at times, like she had too big of a smile. It looked like someone who filled the silence of phone calls. She was here, and then she wasn't, even before she died.

When my mom and dad got divorced, I was too young to notice or understand, but my sister was a teenager and was the one who had to mother our mom. So later, she checked on my mom each day. Yet even she didn't know the extent of our mom's sadness, or the depth of her depression. My aunt, my mom's sister, was busy taking care of my grandma, and both were angry with me for telling her what had happened. They knew my mom was struggling, but no one had told me, and no one seemed to know just how much.

So where could I start to try to understand all this?

My mom had been sick, but there were no medical records to track—no tumor that grows without detection, no virus that moves from organ to organ before causing symptoms to warn you of its presence. Since I needed now to know everything about my mom, everything I could learn, I thought I would need to approach it like a reporter, learn about her last day on earth, and then move backward. My sister had told me our mom had died sometime in the morning. My sister had learned about our mom's death in the late afternoon. I knew my mom had left her car near Bright Angel Lodge and that she had left notes. My sister had said there wasn't much more to say.

At the time, this was enough. I knew there would have been an investigation into my mom's death, that someone at the Grand Canyon would have investigated and documented her death to prove that it was a suicide. When I received a copy of the park service investigative report, it was thirty-six pages long. It documented the investigation, typed in some areas, handwritten in others. There were interviews from a canyon shuttle bus driver and those with my mom's husband and my sister; there were latitude and longitude coordinates; types of helicopters and hours of overtime; photos of suicide notes. There was the search and recovery, and so much more. Maybe if I didn't have the why, the how would lead me there.

The report helped me piece together what happened that night, the night when I was eighteen hundred miles away at a rainy baseball game watching Luke play catcher, and Lucy got so soaked that she wanted to ride in the car home in just a towel—the night Theo climbed an oak tree so tall that I took a photo to send to my mom, but then remembered how she always worried about Theo. I would learn that as I put the kids to bed, my mom likely would have been reading the email I had sent earlier that week. Her husband would later tell rangers he "believed this caused (his wife) to become distressed."

Her husband got into the shower that evening, and when he got out, she was gone. He told rangers that he hadn't worried about my mom when he couldn't find her. My mom was supposed to take her then eighty-nine-year-old mom to the doctor in the morning, and he assumed she had driven to her mom's house in Scottsdale, about thirty minutes away, to stay the night and make it easier in the morning.

My sister would later say she had thought our mom was staying at our grandma's house. My grandma thought she was home with her husband. So no one checked on her that night, they thought she was OK.

At some point, my mom got in to her Jeep and drove 221 miles from Phoenix to the Grand Canyon. She would have had to use her debit card to pay the twenty-five-dollar park entrance fee at a ticket kiosk. Then at some point, she parked in a lot in front of the Bright Angel Lodge. We don't know what time she arrived, if she walked along the canyon, sat among the trees, slept, or a combination of those things.

The report would tell me that at 1:11 A.M. my mother tried to call my sister and then her husband. Neither answered. I would learn that about a week before, my mom had stopped by to see her mom and to give her a turquoise necklace my mom had made, one she had worn frequently. It had natural chunks of turquoise of varying sizes that she found at a gem show in Tucson. She had strung the stones on a thin wire with tiny silver beads between each stone. She had made an almost identical necklace for me, except she used coral, and had given it to me for Christmas a few years prior. My necklace had the tiny silver heart looped into the clasp that my mom notched into all of her jewelry.

In the report, I read that my mom's husband told rangers that his wife had been depressed over her relationship with me, that I had sent emails that said I "forgave" my mom, but that she couldn't forgive herself. He didn't tell the ranger why, but later my sister did. My mom's husband told the ranger that my mom had been depressed recently, but had no history of suicide attempts, had never talked about suicide before, but that the tone she had used when she called that morning was serious. It had scared him.

That night, rangers called my mom's husband again, but noted that he "had difficulty hearing and was intoxicated" so they called my sister and decided "all communication would go through her." They wanted to learn if our mom had been depressed, or shown any signs of suicide.

When I read this part of the report, I learned that my sister told the rangers our mom had been upset about the abuse revelations. She told them that our mom's husband said he had no recollection due to him being an alcoholic, having a stroke and a brain tumor, and being unable to live on his own. My sister said our mom felt "responsible for taking care of (her husband) and at the same time felt horrible for being with him knowing what he did to (me)." My sister said our mom "couldn't live with (her husband) and couldn't live without him."

My sister told rangers that our mom had been attending Saturday night Mass at the Franciscan Renewal Center each week with her sister, our aunt. Our mom had recently told her sister that she wanted to "walk in front of a truck," my sister said, and a few days before she killed herself, she had told my sister that she "felt bad about being happy about anything in life." My sister told rangers that our mom was seeing a therapist to get over feeling responsible for bringing her husband into our lives.

My sister also said she had talked to my mom by phone two or three times a day to check on her, and said our mom had been "overwhelmingly sad." Each of us saw some of the signs, and knew she was sad, that we needed to check on her, but figured it would pass. Our mom was strong, she had dealt with adversity, and she would get through this. It would just take time. None of us, obviously, thought our mom would do what she did.

That night or early morning, our mom wrote a text to my sister, one that wouldn't be sent the day she killed herself because she must have been too far from a cell tower when she tried to send it. The text arrived a few days later after the rangers recovered my mom's cellphone, charged it, and it received a signal.

The text my mom sent my sister from the edge starts: "Hi honey, it's late and I received a very honest and tough email from Laura. I have failed her in all ways as a mom." She told her that all her financial information, her bank account numbers, a copy of the trust, and her passwords, one of which we would find out was *ilikeicecream,* were in a green book on her desk. It ends with: "To all of my grandchildren, Henry, Theo, Luke, Lucy, Jack, Charlie, Thomas, and Violet: you have been the joy of my life. I will miss you and seeing you grow to be beautiful adults. I'm so very sorry to disappoint all of you. In my heart this is not right, but it's all I can do. Please pray for my soul."

It became impossible not to blame myself, impossible to read this text in the ranger report, these words, to not feel immense responsibility for her death. I can remind myself many times over that there isn't one thing that causes someone to kill themselves, that while suicide notes can be helpful to some families, they are written in a moment of extreme distress. Years of research, therapy, and medicine can tell me that I am not to blame. But then I read these words, "I received a very honest email from Laura," and I can't breathe. I have to start all over again, reminding myself that suicide shouldn't be blamed on one thing. I try to remind myself not to be so selfish as to think my mom would kill herself over me. I count backward from ten. The words will always haunt me.

My mom tried calling me the morning she died. I declined the call and sent her a text.

My mom sent a text to me that I didn't receive, or don't remember receiving in those first days after her death, and didn't know existed until her phone was recovered, and the texts were photographed and logged into the ranger report. I read them four years later.

My mom wrote: "Thank you. That could not have been an easy letter to write. I'm sorry that I have not made it clear that I am sorry for my behavior. At first I could not believe the atrocities and abuse that you suffered. This from a man I loved and trusted for 25 years. As it became evident that everything was true that you initially told me I should have made myself more clear that I was sorry for my behavior and lack of support for you and I am sorry I know this may seem too late and I can't change that but know I believe you and I'm sorry I love you and always always will and hope you can forgive me for ever doubting you. Try to be strong. You have a wonderful family and I know John and his family love you. Your dad and sister love you, too. I wish I could take away the pain. I can only try to be here for you if only you will let me. Love always."

If I had received this text on that morning, would it have made a difference? She says she can "try to be here for you if only you will let me." Yet she also wrote suicide notes to say goodbye, contradicting herself. Would I have understood the state of mind my mom was in? Would I have known that it was as urgent as it was? And if I had, could I have done anything? Would I have called my sister? I wonder if my mom's voice would have sounded hollow and emotionless, or halting and cracking.

I imagine the conversation we would have had—I play my imagined apology over and over in my head. I talk her away from the ledge. I talk her home, and I fly home to see her. I get to hug her, I get to make sure she knows I understand how complicated this is for her, that people can be many things, that we are resilient, that we can survive anything. She will get to see her grandchildren who love her more than anything.

I wake up at three A.M. still many nights. I replay this conversation, this conversation that never happened, the one that maybe could have helped her, the one that could have helped me, the one that means she is here, and I am not writing this, not feeling like I do—and then, instead, I count backward from one hundred until I fall back asleep.

The photograph of the text messages on her phone show the people who cared about her. Two texts from me. One from my sister. My mom's best friend, Ellen, who texted, "Do you want me to come pick you up?"

The park ranger's report also archives everything she left behind in her Jeep, a 2002 white Liberty. Each item is lined up on a table or the carpet, photographed, and identified as photos 1–30. Five photos are missing, and in text below it reads, "Intentionally Left Blank." First the missing photos make me think of someone not showing up for yearbook photos and the words "Not pictured" in a silhouette, and I think about what part of my mom's life didn't show up here. I wonder if "intentionally blank" means the rangers didn't put photos there because somehow they liked the contents of my mom's purse in symmetry on page 35, and didn't want to begin them on page 34 and mix them with the photo of her phone, which was found in her jacket pocket. Or maybe they removed the photos when they made a copy of the report for my benefit or that of the family. There are places in the report where rangers detail that they photographed the bag in which they placed my mom's body. Was this bag the photo 10, one of the "intentionally left blanks"? Somehow this feels important, and I let my mind rest here, instead of returning to the words I see in the photos of the texts my mother wrote.

What I find on pages 34 and 35 capture the detritus of life of a middle-aged woman, the contents of what was in my mom's straw purse. I laughed at the thought, thinking about all the women's magazines that like to detail the contents of a celebrity's purse, one that obviously has been carefully curated to contain items they promote—the drugstore mascara next to the fifty-dollar lipstick with a clever name for *red,* all inside either a bag that probably costs as much as my mortgage payment, or something chic and cheap.

My mom's purse is different—it's her straw summer bag. It's laid flat in photo 25, noting that it was found in her Jeep. Photo 26 is her red leather wallet, and the next photos, 27 through 30, show what was inside. It contained: a Burt's Bees lip balm in burgundy, maybe the same one I had put in her stocking a few months before for Christmas; eight $20 bills, three $5 bills, and seven $1 bills; a Sacagawea coin, six quarters, four dimes, two nickels, and three pennies; keys to her Jeep with a Fry's VIP store card—her car key and three keys, including one to my Phoenix house where we hadn't lived for a few months; a four-ounce container of Eucerin hand cream; two black ballpoint pens; one blue ballpoint pen; reading glasses; a miniature navy-blue composition book with notes written in cursive to her family; and an Altoids tin with three Tylenols and two Imodium tablets. In her Jeep: a dog ramp and an ironing board. The report, in photo 21, shows her iPhone 4 with its lime-green plastic case with a photo of the canyon with a brilliant blue sky and the description, "Photo of Grand Canyon, believed to be the location where she jumped." It also shows a screen grab with my last words to my mom, typed hastily into my phone at 8:10 A.M. that day: "I love you, Mom. Crazy busy workday. Hard to break away to talk. But know I love you." It now is preserved for me, for always. I sent it too late. She maybe never saw it.

I think about what we could have done, should have done, but didn't. I think about what was.

At some point, my mom wrote notes in a composition book, a book no taller than six inches that looked like a miniature version of the old-school notebooks, with her name written in cursive with a ballpoint pen on the front. We don't know if she wrote in the notebook while sitting in her car, somewhere outside when it was still light, or sometime before at home. Did she sit in her Jeep and write the notes by the overhead light in the night? Did she wait until the sun rose and then write them that morning? The text she sent to my sister indicating she had all her passwords and finances in one place, and had recently moved her house into a trust for us, seemed to indicate she'd thought about some of this earlier. But we know that the act of suicide is typically more impulsive, so she could have been feeling low, but she could have also been feeling a little better at times. She wrote in blue ballpoint pen, which I presume is one of the pens that was catalogued from her purse. Or did she write the notes weeks ago?

She left five notes, each inside the small wide-ruled composition book, which also contains miscellaneous scribbles: the address for the neuro rehab, presumably where her husband had been attending, and the names of a counselor, a psychologist, a spiritual counselor, and an email address for an Al-Anon sponsor. There are notes that were maybe or maybe not written during an Al-Anon meeting she attended, as she had struggled with her husband's drinking; sometimes it would get so bad she would go to Al-Anon, and then she would drop off. "Topic is humility. You're next. Dick is an alcoholic." She writes what appears to be instructions for her husband, maybe taken at her last meeting? "Each person when their ticket is drawn talks about what they want with sobriety. Think about it so you can talk." I try to make sense of something that makes no sense. She wrote her Apple password and her cellphone number password, things she didn't mention in the text.

The scribbles might have felt inconsequential, simply things to remember, if they hadn't been followed by suicide notes to her family. The suicide notes are written in cursive, some on back-to-back pages, the pen's indentation felt through the other side of the pages.

To her husband:

"Dick, I love you & am so sorry that this will hurt you more than anyone. You have been my gift. Do not blame yourself or anyone else. This is all my fault. I was too proud to admit I needed help a very long time ago. Please keep going to AA. Walter will be a good sponsor and friend. You are a strong man. You deserve the joy & freedom of sobriety. I'll love you always."

To her mom:

"Mom, please forgive me. I've made such a mess of my life. You, my dear mom are so wonderful & the most loving person I know. Please don't try to find blame—I believe I have been sick for a very long time & didn't take care of me. I love you and will always regret the mistakes I have made. Please continue to show your strength & love with my family. Always love you."

To her sister:

"Please take care of my family. You have inspired me with your kindness and spirituality. You have guided and protected me through life. I can never thank you enough for always being my big sis and loving me and my family. They will need you now as they always have. Don't search for blame—this is my fault for not taking care of me and being too proud to ask for help. You my dear sister will always be in my heart, Love you."

To my sister:

"This is so hard. To my beautiful daughter, forgive me. I will love you always. You have been my rock when I should have been yours. You are such a wonderful person providing love for your family with grace & joy. I am so proud of you. Each of your children are a reflection of the love you shower upon them. Be good to yourself and please forgive me for this life I have left. Love you, Mom."

To me:

"I can never make things right & no matter what I say or do you will never believe me. Maybe you can get on with living now. You have so much to live for and your family needs you. I do, too. You are a beautiful woman with so much creativity, joy & care for your family & friends. You never fail to amaze me with how you handle life with such ease. Be kind to yourself. Love, Mom."

The report documents that the first call to the Grand Canyon rangers came that April morning at 7:15: A woman was threatening suicide. My mom had called her husband, telling him this was it, she was ending it all. She told him she was at the canyon, before the call ended abruptly. He called 911 and the operator connected him to the park service. The ranger who answered the phone learned my mom had driven a white Jeep Liberty, that she had last mentioned she was at the Trailview Overlook, and that she was sixty-six and it was possible she would be wearing tan pants and a light jacket, the last thing her husband saw her in the day before. The rangers then notified all the shuttle bus drivers and within a few minutes, a driver told rangers that the woman matching that description was dropped at Trailview Overlook. By 7:35, two more rangers quickly began searching along the South Rim, hiking the Rim Trail along the canyon from the village to the overlook, with more rangers pulled in at 8:00 that morning. By 9:00, they'd found my mom's car and the suicide notes, and a note that said "Call Dick" and gave their home phone number.

Two rangers then used binoculars from different areas to see if they could spot her near the Trailview Overlook area. They called the helicopter crew to see if they might be able to do a quick flyover of the area to find her. The weather was windy with scattered showers, a storm moving south. By 10:45 that morning, rangers had launched helicopter 368 with three crew members and were heading toward the Trailview area. Within fifteen minutes, they'd spotted a body and recorded the location. N 36°03'40.61", W 112°08'45.35", below the overlook area, maybe 100 feet down.

By coincidence, one of my friends was at the Grand Canyon that day. Megan—whom I have known almost twenty years, meeting her when she was just out of college as my intern—and three of her friends had hiked down the South Kaibab Trail the day before and stayed at Phantom Ranch at the bottom of the canyon. They were hiking up Bright Angel Trail late that Thursday morning. It was so windy and gray, she said, not quite raining, but misting as they walked the switchbacks, and they spotted a yellow helicopter hovering overhead.

She asked a ranger what the helicopter was doing. He told Megan that a person had died and they were trying to recover the body. Megan said that as she hiked out, she prayed both silently and out loud that this person was at peace. The weather grew worse, the wind stronger, and the helicopter needed to turn back.

As Megan climbed the switchbacks over and over, she could see a rocky space below where the helicopter had hovered. Each time she passed, she said a silent prayer.

The helicopter crew noted that it appeared that rangers would be able to hike to my mom's body. A ranger called the county medical examiner's office to inform the examiner of the death and request permission to remove the body. It was granted. At 12:30 that afternoon, two rangers hiked down Bright Angel Trail and cut across the canyon, off the main trail, where they walked another half mile through dirt that was beginning to turn to mud, between scrubby bushes, to reach my mom. One of the rangers put my mom's body in a bag. The ranger zipped my mom's body into a second bag and then placed the bag inside a net. The trail was too rugged to safely carry her out—they decided a helicopter would be better. But the weather was too foggy, too gray to fly that day. He secured the bag to a skinny pine tree for the night and took photos to document the recovery. They decided to return the next day when the weather was better, and they hiked out. The temperature that night dropped to twenty-eight degrees.

By 3:00 P.M., rangers had sent a Phoenix police officer to tell my mom's husband that they had found the body of a woman matching my mom's description. The ranger called to also talk to my mom's husband, but said after the initial hello, he dropped the phone and never returned. At 4:30 that afternoon, the ranger informed my sister that they had found our mom.

The next morning, the weather cleared just after ten, and one of the rangers who had hiked down to find my mom hiked back to her body. Somehow, when I read that he was the same ranger, I was relieved, comforted, if that makes any sense. I felt a strong sense that the rangers cared about her. He waited next to the bag that held her body until the same helicopter was able to take off from the nearby helipad at the rim, and soon hovered above.

Megan had stayed the night at the rim of the canyon, and just after breakfast, she and her friends headed to the Kolb Studio. It's a place where Emery and Ellsworth Kolb first set up a tent in 1904 and took some of the most well-known and memorable photos of early tourists at the canyon— black-and-white snapshots of families riding mules down the Bright Angel Trail. Later the tent would become a cabin built over into the wall with a darkroom and an auditorium where visitors could watch a movie the brothers made of the Colorado River. There were even stories that they would hike down four miles to Indian Gardens, where water flowed readily, to help develop their photos. In many ways, what the brothers saw through their camera shaped the nation's view of the Grand Canyon. Emery and his family owned the cabin until he died in 1976 and the Grand Canyon Association renovated the cabin. It grew into a five-story structure and became a bookstore and gallery. It's on the National Register of Historic Places to preserve the brothers' photos, serving as a lookout onto Bright Angel Trail with a small window on the west wall facing the trail.

On this day, the rain and wind had subsided, and the sky was so blue, Megan said. She stood along the rim with her friends and watched two condors swooping over the canyon. Condors had almost become extinct before being placed on the endangered species list in 1967. A captive breeding program in 1983 introduced six condors to the wild just north of the Grand Canyon. The park service now counts seventy-one, though often visitors think they see a condor but they actually see the turkey vulture, much more common. The sight of a real condor is amazing, with its wingspan about ten feet across—four feet longer than the vulture. Even from a distance over the majestic canyon, the condors are amazing to see.

The helicopter lowered a basket to the ranger, who then loaded her body into the basket. Watching the birds, Megan said, she almost didn't notice the yellow helicopter, even in the clear sky. On the rim, Megan said, people immediately realized what the hanging basket meant. She looked to the trail below as people paused in their hikes. And she looked around, as people turned attention from the condors to the recovery, spiritually and emotionally present to witness the leaving. Some crossed themselves and prayed, Megan said, or stood quiet in a way that's rare for crowds and even more so for vacationers. She didn't know who was in the basket, couldn't have known, but she said the Our Father and the Hail Mary silently. The helicopter, she said, felt like the only sound in the world as it flew away.

The helicopter returned to its pad where the medical examiner was waiting. The park service logged everything in a very thorough report, from the seventy-nine hours of national park employees' time at a cost of $1,975, the four hours of overtime hazardous pay costs at $140, supplies at $350, and the helicopter time, which was $2,381.50, which means they used either a medium or heavy helicopter for .7 hours. It took eighteen people to bring my mom home.

Eighteen people cared about her when they didn't know her, when she wasn't here anymore to let her know. I can only hope that anyone who thinks they are alone, whose brain won't let them see clearly, whose depression has taken hold, knows about the eighteen people and that someone else is out there, someone else cares.

When I think about my mom's death, about the very public place she died, about the spot where she wanted to spend her last moments, I sometimes feel less anxious about it all. I can almost take a full breath. I become pragmatic, which I can be in the best of times. In the past two decades, my mom had climbed the steps at Chichen Itza in Mexico and crossed through the locks from a ship on the Panama Canal, zip-lined through the forests of Belize and come face-to-face with a bear on a trail in Alaska. She'd sailed a catamaran in the clear waters of the Virgin Islands, hosted Camp Grandma with campfires among the pine trees at Mormon Lake, and dug in the impossibly hard rocky mountainside of her Phoenix home to plant cacti and irises, and nurtured a mum she'd received forty-one years earlier when her father died. Yet the canyon remained her favorite place, something almost spiritual for her—a place she found beauty, where she had watched the sun rise for Easter Mass, where nature brought her comfort. It was a place where a ranger watched over her body, where strangers prayed for her. I know we are not supposed to say that people who kill themselves found peace, because that could appear that we are glorifying suicide, or justifying it in a way, and we are not. But I guess what I mean is that in the best of times, I feel comfort knowing she is no longer in pain.

Chapter 10

My Mother's Daughter

MY MOM DIDN'T grow up in Arizona; she was a girl from a town of 541 in Cedar Rapids, Nebraska, a town not far from many other small towns that had a church and a tavern and a school, about 140 miles west of Omaha. Her dad went to college to become a dentist in the 1940s, then opened a bar instead of a dental practice. Bill's Tavern was a place that exists only in the few stories my mom shared, and whose name was on an ashtray that somehow survived for decades of moves. My mom's father wasn't young when she was born. He was my grandma's second husband; her first died in World War II, about a year after the couple had their first baby, a girl. The story goes that my grandma was not even twenty and had a one-year-old, and was living in a small town. She needed someone to take care of her and her baby, and Bill, two decades older, needed someone to take care of him. They married that year and soon after had my mom. Two years later they had a son.

The family of five lived above the tavern or they didn't live above the tavern, because no one alive knows or wants to talk about it. But my mom had told stories of her and her little brother sneaking maraschino cherries from the bar, and my mom knowing how to tie them with her tongue as a kid. She and her sister used to dress up and pretend they were nuns, putting white underpants on their heads and then a black slip over it to make a habit. My grandma would draw the curtains closed, worried the Lutheran neighbors would think poorly of her raising Catholic girls who played dress-up as nuns. Did they live above the tavern or didn't they? I asked my sister. My mom last visited Nebraska sometime in the 2000s—she had photos of an old farmhouse. Was it hers? Or her aunt's house? And does it matter? In the last census in 2010, Cedar Rapids had 382 residents.

My mom remembers her father always smelling of smoke, either from his own cigarettes, or from working the bar, and most likely both. After decades of smoking, he started coughing more often than he didn't. Doctors told the family his lungs were closing and emphysema was making it harder for him to breathe. They told him to move to Arizona, where the dry, hot air would open his lungs. Moving west was common advice in the late 1950s for anyone with asthma or breathing problems. Arizona was a place my mom's family knew only from Westerns. They bought a two-bedroom, single-wide trailer in Chandler, a town at that time mostly known for cotton fields and citrus groves in a suburb of Phoenix. My mom and her siblings went to Catholic school.

My mom remembers these years as some of her favorite even though she didn't have many friends yet, starting high school as the new, shy, pale girl with carrot-orange hair and black cat-eyed glasses. My mom smiled when she told the stories, even the part about sharing a tiny room with her sister and little brother. She loved getting off the school bus and walking to find her dad sitting in his recliner each day. He no longer could work, and his worsening lungs meant he spent most of his time in the house. She would sit with him, listening to his stories, of life before her or her mom, of days on a farm, building his own boat, fishing, and later tending bar.

When my mom graduated from high school, she followed her older sister to study to become an X-ray technician at a school connected to a hospital in Phoenix. It wouldn't take as long as nursing school and it seemed the logical step, she said. She didn't know what she wanted to do. She lived in a dorm with her sister and two other girls, making grilled-cheese sandwiches with an iron. I don't know why that is the one story I remember.

As a child, my own life was unremarkable in most ways.

My mom and dad married when she was twenty and he was twenty-two. She would have been two months pregnant with my sister on their wedding day that February. My sister was born later that year, and three and a half years later, I was born; the next year, my mom's father died.

After she had my sister, my mom worked at a nearby hospital, and a friend of my dad's mom lived with them and took care of the baby. When I was born, my mom decided to stay home. They bought a ranch house in a solidly middle-class neighborhood on the west side of Phoenix. My dad worked as a forensic scientist for the state, leaving the house at seven each morning and coming home at five every evening. He would work the crossword puzzle from the morning paper while my mom made dinner and we set the table, and dinner started at six each night. It was expected that friends knew not to ring the doorbell or call during dinner. We sat in the same spots each night, my sister to my left, my dad to my right, and my mom across from me, closest to the kitchen, of course. My dad's mom, who was born in Arizona to Mexican parents, taught my red-haired, blue-eyed, freckled, Irish mom to fry chile rellenos and beef tacos, to make tamales and menudo. They folded her so close into the family.

While we were growing up, my mom sewed our Halloween costumes and her own evening gown for the annual charity ball at the Elks Lodge, where my dad was not only member forty-six but also the Exalted Ruler, the head of the lodge. She led the Camp Fire Girls' Bluebird troop, hosted swim parties, and gathered the neighborhood families for our dogs to race through obstacles in a field behind our house. She once moved all the living room furniture in our sunken living room and taught the neighborhood moms how to do the hustle. Later she went to community college so she could become a registered nurse. She wanted to go back to work as we got older.

Things were good until they weren't.

Before my mom killed herself, did I look at my childhood in a different way? Was I able to just see the good, the family that felt tightly stitched together? Was I able now to brush aside any of the bad? Were things that seemed quirky in my childhood actually missed signs? Does the present distort the lens through which we see the past? As a kid, I didn't even see the signs, or didn't notice them as something to be alarmed about. Doesn't everyone's mom start a fire in the bathroom trash, and say she wants to burn down the house?

My sister and I were taught to be perfect girls. Anything less than an A+ meant we had failed. Coming home with a simple A filled me with fear. We were rewarded for doing well, not asking questions, and smiling when we met strangers. We weren't raised to point out anything that didn't feel right. If it wasn't your business, you didn't talk about it. But I remember making a list of things as a child, things I wanted. I remember writing, "Get all A+'s. Win my butterfly race in my swim meets. Protect Mom. Don't disappoint Dad."

Was there something underneath that I had seen but not recognized? When my parents got divorced, my mom stayed in the house we grew up in with my sister and me and our dog; my dad moved to an apartment near the mall and became a Wednesday-night and every-other-weekend dad. I was ten and my sister was starting her freshman year of high school. My mom's weight dropped. She worked nights as an emergency room nurse. That year, we didn't see her so much. She would get up to say goodbye to us before we left for school, but she would be gone when we got home, returning after we were asleep.

My mom was sinking further away, in a way so slow, it was unnoticeable. As a child, I didn't notice any signs at first, or I didn't realize they were signs of depression. I just saw less of her at first—she was sleeping more when she was home or worrying obsessively that she wasn't safe when she was alone and my sister and I were at our dad's house for the weekend. But she still went to work, and I was busy with student council or softball. I didn't notice. I had a nice house, clothes, food—it wasn't as if we were neglected. We saw my dad regularly, he helped me with algebra on Wednesdays and then took me to play Pac-Man. My parents never said a bad word about the other to us.

My mom found religion in the Franciscan Renewal Center or the Casa. The church began in a former dusty dude ranch in an area that ten years later would be incorporated as Paradise Valley, home to professional basketball players and retired baseball players, and some of the nicest homes near Phoenix. The church hosts spiritual retreats, mass, and religious education classes; it offers counseling and respite. It works in cooperation with the Catholic diocese, but remains apart, allowing it to "welcome all," open to any faith. The church, in the early 1980s, also embraced singing and arm movements that reminded my sister and me of aerobics. We once were sent out of mass to sit in the car because we hadn't been able to stop laughing in church, and our mom finally made us leave. We were more than fine with it.

My mom joined a singles group. She stayed up too late at her sister's house, drinking wine and telling us to get ourselves ready for school on our own the next day. Her sister thought some time in nature would be good for my mom. Her sister owned a cabin about an hour south of the Grand Canyon, the place where we spent some of our summers, a quiet and secluded cabin that was a good place to escape summer's heat. We skipped rocks across Mormon Lake, built forts in a forest, and learned to cross-country ski. Because we grew up in the desert, we could spend afternoons on the back deck, simply watching chipmunks and squirrels and waiting for the deer.

After the divorce, my mom's sister promised her a trip to the Grand Canyon, something to look forward to, something that would be good for her. My aunt knew the canyon well; my mom had never been. My dad stayed with us for a week, and my mom and her sister drove to the canyon, camping along the rim in the back of my aunt's Bronco; they swore they saw a UFO after a bottle of wine. Then they hiked to the bottom of the canyon along the Bright Angel Trail, carrying a tent and sleeping bags. The details as I remember: They brought their own food and ate a Hickory Farms log of salami, and my mom said her sweat began to smell like salami. People kept asking about my mom and her sister's relationship, as if it was odd for two women to hike the canyon alone in the 1980s. They said they were sisters, which some took to mean they were nuns, and others took to mean they were married. My mom loved both interpretations equally.

What I remember at this time was a mom who never said she was tired, but she must have been. She worked the three-to-eleven P.M. shift, and raised us girls. My dad in no way would have been considered absent, but the responsibility for our lives, for doctors' appointments, field trip permission slip signatures, new sneakers, haircuts, and swim team sign-up, fell to her, which maybe was normal in the 1980s for a single mom.

She took a self-defense class and bought a handgun. She joined the Phoenix Ski Club, known mostly at the time as a place for singles, and she even learned to ski.

She began to go on dates, so many dates. My sister and I would watch the men come to the door from a chair we pulled up to the window in my sister's bedroom, which faced the street. There was the teacher who bent down and talked to us like we were five. We were so offended. The man who came in a three-piece plaid suit for dinner on a Phoenix summer night.

My mom's weight continued to drop. She no longer had cheeks—this is what I could see, as my mom withered away. What I didn't know was that at some point during this time, after her shift at the hospital, she drove to a parking lot with the handgun she had bought for self-defense. And this is maybe what happened and maybe not, the pieces get put together as we each tried to find out how things ended this way. How does someone go from happy to suicide? Or what we thought was happy, what we missed, what remained. My sister told me this story sometime after the funeral when we looked for clues. We discussed the day our mom set the house on fire in a bathroom garbage can shortly after our dad left. My mom put it out before it spread.

Soon after the fire, our grandma and her grumpy miniature schnauzer, Shone, moved in with us. My grandma slept on the pull-out couch in the den and seemed to make ham for dinner at least twice a week. We were told that our grandma was staying with us because she needed help. But then why did she leave her husband in their condominium in Chandler? I never asked—I was still too little and naïve to understand. After a few months, our grandma moved back to her house. I figured my grandma must have been better.

In our own ways after my mom died, we each tried to understand what had happened and what we knew. My sister said our grandma told her that our mom was put in a hospital or rather some type of institution at some point before she married our dad, but when I asked my sister later about this, she said she didn't remember. Maybe that wasn't what our grandma told her, she said. And the thing with suicide is this: Everyone has their own part of a story, and many don't want to share. There is shame for some, and for others there is blame. Many don't want to talk about it, they don't want to answer questions, or even remember the past. There's no one who has the answer and sometimes the bits they have, they lock inside. Or they remember the way they can, or want. They want to protect the memory of the person they love.

On a spring break a few years after my mom died, I drove with Lucy to the bottom tip of Florida to see my mom's best friend from when I was a kid. Nancy and my mom were practically inseparable for most of my childhood. Born two days apart, they'd had matching Dorothy Hamill haircuts and New Balance running shoes; they were moms of Lisa and Laura, and Karan and Christy. They lived seventeen houses apart on Denton Lane and would meet in the middle to run three miles each night and figure out life. They spent so much time together that it was my mom who noticed that Karan wasn't well as a little girl, and suggested Nancy take her to be tested for cystic fibrosis, which she was later diagnosed with.

Nancy had a sign on the door to welcome us, and she'd set up a room for Lucy with a bunk bed. Lucy fell in love with Nancy, and so did I. We walked the two blocks to the ocean together. I spent far too much time wanting her to be my mom, and forgetting to look at how she was just Nancy, not my mom—similar, yes, but herself. We talked about depression, something we both have known. I saw Karan, the little girl who has cystic fibrosis and is now a beautiful woman; she had a double lung transplant twenty-two years ago. My mom had worried about Karan for years after she lost contact with Nancy, donating to cystic fibrosis organizations in her memory, fearing Karan hadn't survived the disease.

Nancy and I sat next to the pool, our feet in the water that felt warm to the Midwesterners we were now. Nancy, who has lived in Florida for four decades, wore a long-sleeved shirt. Lucy was with us and leaned over to me and whispered, "I keep almost calling her Grandma. It's just, you know, she looks so much like her and she is fun and silly, too."

I smiled and nodded.

"I know, Lu, I do."

And maybe that was why we were there—leaving Ohio and driving through Kentucky and Tennessee, North Carolina and South, through the corner of Georgia to reach this quiet barrier island in Florida.

From the side, I saw it, too—my mom in Nancy's face. And there she was, watching us and smiling, just like my mom would have. Was it weird that we were sitting with her, staying with Nancy?

I hadn't seen Nancy in decades. Nancy had written a note on my mom's obituary tribute online and we later found each other through Facebook. She knew I was missing my mom, and that Lucy was missing her grandma. "What if you came out for a while?" she had said. And so we did.

I marveled at the intense similarities that remained between my mom and Nancy. One night, after Lucy had gone to bed, Nancy and I sat on her white slipcovered couch, and we both wished so much that my mom were there with us, laughing and remembering life on Denton Lane. She told me stories of how the day Christy and I started school, my mom called and said, "Nancy, we need jobs." We talked about how they went on runs together because it was one time they could get away from their children.

"Did you ever see anything?" I asked.

"See what?"

"My mom—did you ever see anything, signs that something wasn't right?" I asked.

"We talked every day," she said, "but it was the seventies, and people didn't talk about things like that. We didn't talk about feelings. We talked about crafts and what we were making for dinner, about what we were doing with you girls. One day on our run, she said she wanted to buy a gun. I laughed and said, 'Things with your husband can't be that bad,' thinking she was joking."

Nancy paused for a minute, and I wondered where this was going.

"Your mom said it wouldn't be for him," she said. "I never asked, never called her, never wondered what she meant. Friends didn't talk about things like that. Maybe I could have helped her."

A few years later, Nancy and her family moved across town and later would be transferred through the air force to Florida.

"I didn't think about that conversation," she said, "until you told me how your mom died. I just didn't know to ask. I wish I had."

I scooted closer on the couch, and laid my head on Nancy's shoulder. I tried really hard not to pretend she was my mom, but just my friend.

Later that week, just as Lucy and I were loading up the car for the trip home, I told Nancy I had something for her.

I gave her the coral necklace with the silver beads that my mom made for me, the one that matched the turquoise necklace, the one with the little silver heart looped into the clasp. I wanted her to have it. I like to think my mom would have liked that.

I WROTE QUESTIONS in the back of a little composition book, things I wanted to know from my dad. Did Mom ever seem sad? Did you think she was depressed? Did she ever say she wanted to kill herself? Do you know about her staying in a hospital before you got married? My dad is someone who is measured with his words, speaking only when necessary, and never about others unless it's something good. If you say something bad about someone, he doesn't listen or acknowledge it. You can sit next to my dad and watch basketball for hours without words and it's not awkward, it's just who he is. If you don't tell him something, he doesn't ask. It's not his business. Talking about feelings with my dad is not something I had ever done, so this would not be easy.

When I last visited Phoenix, Lucy and I stayed at a resort with a big pool, and she invited her best friends from when we lived there. They went to explore and my dad and I sat in the hotel room, and I told him I had some questions. He nodded, acknowledging what I said, which made me think maybe this time he would talk. And so I decided it might be OK.

I had told my dad that I wanted to write about my mom, about her suicide, about me. When I asked my dad about my mom, and whether he remembered her being depressed, he said he understood: "Why don't you let things be, Laura."

I told him that writing about it might help, not me, but others.

"Your sister has dealt with this and bringing it back up won't do any good," he said. "And that's how I feel, too."

His wife interrupted us.

"My brother killed himself," she said. "I blamed myself forever. He always called me before he left work to say, 'I love you, sis.' And one night he didn't."

Looking back, she said, that was unusual. "I could have called him, I could have checked," she said, and her voice disappeared. The next morning, she had watched a medical helicopter lift off and learned later that her brother had been in it.

"It took a long time, you know, for me to not think it was my fault, that I could have done something," she said. "It's been decades, a long time for me to know he's gone. And that's it."

My dad didn't say anything; he looked at the ground.

"So, was she depressed?" I asked my dad.

"You need to let this go," he said. "And no. I don't remember any of it."

I wondered if he felt guilt, about leaving my mom, about my mom remarrying a man who raped me, about all of it. Was this hard on him? I thought about how when I was barely five, my dad's brother's wife killed herself. We never talked about it, and I didn't even know that was how she died until more than a decade later, after I had graduated from college and spent a summer with my cousin. She told me that's how her mom had died.

I'd been so busy feeling bad over losing my mom that sometimes I forgot that all of us knew her, all of us didn't see her growing sicker in front of us. My dad didn't see it. My sister didn't. My dad was married again, to his third wife, an incredibly kind woman with three grown kids of her own, a woman who loves her grandchildren and counts my sister's children and mine as hers. Together, she and my dad go to church each week, and believe deeply in the Bible. My dad, who for so long shunned religion and believed in the Big Bang and things with a scientific basis, had changed his beliefs.

"If you ask for forgiveness and accept the Lord as your Savior, I would feel a lot better," he said to me.

I told him we should think about where to take Lucy to dinner. He suggested the Cheesecake Factory, and soon we were eating a Thai salad, a cheeseburger, prime rib, and Chicken alfredo, as if nothing or this conversation ever happened.

No one wants to talk about it. They don't want to answer questions, or even remember the past. And maybe that is best.

I was certain for years that the last letter my mom wrote had a stamp with the painting of the Grand Canyon on it. So certain that I never even checked. So certain that I couldn't even look at it. Until one day I did. And the canyon looked, well, short. Turns out, it was Cathedral Rock in Sedona, according to the U.S. Postal Service, which released the stamp in celebration of the state's centennial. And so facts are our own, as are truths. I think of one of my favorite lines from a favorite writer: "We tell ourselves stories in order to live."[1]

Stories change over the years, with memory, maybe, or for survival. There are parts to my mom's story that we all have or hold on to, but don't share. So none of us can see all the contours and the full texture of this story, this woman, this life. We just have our disappointments, our myths, and our guilt. And then there is my grandma who shooed me away at my mom's funeral. So how do I ask her what happened, the parts of the story she knows, her truth? I wrote my aunt a letter, asking for answers, but have received none. And there are stories that change over the years. Memory or survival?

Five years later, I still want to ask again what happened. Maybe with time, distance, people can talk. I am still sad, of course, but it feels different. When my mom first died, it felt like waves, and I was in a rowboat. All I could do was bail out the water to not sink. Not try to get anywhere, just not drown. Now there are waves, but they are small. Or smaller.

So maybe they feel different now, too. Maybe I do.

One day my sister, while cleaning out my mom's house, was asked by my stepfather to try on our mom's bras and show them to him. She didn't go to my mom's house alone again, but would drop off groceries weekly for our stepfather because she thought my mom would want that. She is the one who was called three months later when the newspapers were piled up in front of the house. Our stepfather was dead.

There is the silver bracelet my mom bought on a trip through the Navajo Nation one year, a bracelet she wore with several others on her right arm every day, including the day she died. My sister sent the bracelet to me along with a few other things from our mom, including the gold loop earrings our mom wore that day. I began wearing this simple bracelet on my right wrist, too, a way to keep my mom close. But there was a bend in it, and I couldn't stop thinking about how my mom must have landed on her right side. I thought about how when my sister talked to the medical examiner, she kept saying our mom was "very broken." I tried not to think about it, but anytime I saw a ledge or a fall—in a virtual reality demonstration at work or the drop in a scene in *True Grit*—I no longer could think or breathe. I always had thought of my mom falling in slow motion, of it happening so slowly. But that isn't true, she would have hit the ground within three seconds. I needed to know how she landed— I needed to know if the bend in the bracelet was from her last day.

I received another report, this one from the Office of the Medical Examiner in Coconino County where she died. The twelve injuries specified included multiple skull fractures, mid–cervical spinal fracture, abrasions, contusions, and lacerations, as well as fractures to the left side of her body. There was no mention of her right side, and I knew the bend in the bracelet must have been simply from my mom squeezing it to fit on and off her wrist, and somehow I took comfort in this small detail. I read through the autopsy report, which went into detail about the injuries to my mom. The toxicology screen showed the absence of any drugs or alcohol, and the only stimulant found in her was caffeine. The last line of the report says, "The manner of death is suicide."

Her body was cremated and her ashes were shared by my mom's husband, my aunt and grandmother, my sister and me.

I have spread my mom's ashes in many places she loved: in the Phoenix Mountains Preserve near her home, among the pine trees in the highest hills in Corsica, in the crowded square of St. Peter inside the Vatican, to where she spent her last moments at the Grand Canyon.

While researchers say most suicides are impulsive, my mom's life now seemed to have left an obvious trail.

Despite all the research, there still isn't a proven formula that can predict precisely who is going to kill themselves and who won't, which interventions work, or work for a while, and which don't, which words might save someone one day only to have them slip away the next. It doesn't make any sense why one person who demonstrates all the risk factors lives and another doesn't.

The only person who can explain is gone. So we are left to guess, to piece together what we can. None of us have all the pieces. The wreckage of my stepfather's behavior left our family in a state of strain. We aren't sharing information or being as honest with one another as we might have been. Something the priest told me stuck: All families are difficult, he told me. Some families just know it, and others don't.

Chapter 11

Moving Forward

MY KIDS HAVE learned in their own ways to try to understand how their grandma ended her life, as well as how she lived it. They were lucky that she had lived close to them since Henry was one, and was there the day each of the others was born. She was there, just to tell them she loved them, to make them feel safe, and to tell them she was there. I think they knew that all the way into their cores.

Henry, my eldest, who even as a teenager would drop everything he was doing when my mom would stop by, smiles when he talks about her. He's a senior in college now, and still has a wallet-sized card she made for him with her phone number when we moved, a photo of her yellow Lab on it, and a handwritten note: "Always remember, Grandma loves you. Call me anytime."

Theo, who was just old enough to understand how she died, is now a freshman in college, and the one who sometimes shares stories about her that even I didn't know—how she made chocolate chip cookie bowls for ice cream when he stayed the night at her house, for example. He's recounted the way we described suicide in the days after my mom died: He and his father and I lay in bed, the quilt wrinkling in spots. We explained that for some, life is very hard. It's like walking a very long time, going over mountains and making it farther than you thought you could. Sometimes you can stop and rest, other times you cannot. You just keep going, and she got tired, just too tired to keep going. Her brain told her she couldn't go anymore, and she didn't know where to look.

Luke is a senior in high school and rarely talks about her, but as he learned to drive, he teased me that I drive exactly like my mom: slow and deliberate, with the radio turned down, and I say the exact phrases she would say to me: "Drive carefully. You have precious cargo." I was surprised to read one of his college application essays was about his grandma, and how in the past seven years he has learned to talk about suicide.

Lucy talks about my mom with such a deep sense of closeness and connection that it can surprise me that my mom has been gone longer than she was here for Lucy. At thirteen, she often asks about my relationship with my mom at this age. Lucy wore a locket for a while. When I opened it, it had a photo of herself in it, which made me laugh. Until I saw that the photo on the other side was my mom. Lucy always wanted to be next to her grandma.

ON A LATE-SUMMER night in 2018, Lucy, then twelve years old, and I went to the canyon.

It was a night without moonlight—we could just see a blanket of stars, more stars than sky it seemed. At night, the canyon is just a deep, dark hole, and in some ways it feels more impressive than in the daylight, the emptiness of it all—just as the canyon is so unknowable that geologists and scientists continue to study it and might never know how it began. I believe the same might be true about my life, and my mom. I'm still figuring out how to be OK with that.

I brought Lucy to this place to show her the beauty and the quiet, the arc of time, the way something as immutable as rock looks completely different in the shifting light, to witness what it suggests about the grand design of the world, to feel forces older and stronger than the earth itself, and to accept the vastness of things we cannot know.

And so I tried to learn more as I worked to tell my mom's story. People sometimes ask if writing is healing, and while the act itself wasn't for me, I do realize that as I wrote and shared, something was lifted. But to say that I wrote one thing and then things were better would be an oversimplification. It was, however, one step forward.

Just as I feared I was like my mom, I feared my children might be like me. I worried about the perfect one who seemed like nothing was ever wrong. I worried about the one who sometimes seemed troubled. I worried about the one who never talked about my mom or her suicide, and the one who cried at night about it. Was I worrying about the wrong one at the wrong time? Did I need to worry about any of them? I had read that according to suicide researchers, each suicide affects more than 150 people, meaning each death has tentacles long enough to touch family, friends, workplaces, and whole communities.[1] I also read that family members with a relative who died by suicide can be at a higher risk for suicide than others. For my children, and my own sanity, perhaps, the only way to feel safe was to write, to understand why my mom killed herself. The brain isn't built for this unknown. Many of us crave order and logic and will travel to the edge of the earth to understand "the why" of a given event or phenomenon. We want facts that lead to answers, resolutions, and on to endings.

But suicide is frustrating in that way: Only one person "gets" an ending; the rest of us are left with a story abandoned mid-sentence. So, part of needing to understand my mom's death, specifically, was tied up in needing to understand more broadly how the human animal, which usually fights fiercely in body and mind to stay alive, can turn on itself and not only choose to die, but make it happen.

As someone who tells stories for a living, I think facts and details can give order to things. They may not explain things entirely, but they are calming.

I wanted to perhaps not only know why my mom did it, but guard against myself doing it, too. And so slowly the question flipped: "Why am I here?," not "Why am I here, but why isn't she?"

And once I began to feel OK. It was important to not just feel OK, but show that I was OK.

One winter night in 2016, I went to pick up Theo from a party. His list of grievances on my parenting ran long.

"You're always in my business. You're always trying to figure out what I'm doing. Stop asking if I'm OK. Stop asking if something's wrong," he said, and it went on. I mostly ignored it, knowing this was a teenage brain. I tried not to show any emotion, knowing it would be easiest for both of us this way. I looked straight ahead, following the dotted lines dividing the street. I had planned to listen, and not engage, knowing he would eventually stop. I also was once a teen who snuck out and did things it was best my parents didn't know. It made me a boring college student ("Oh no, thanks, I've already done that"). But Theo was angry that night. It filled the minivan.

He said with all the bravado of someone who thinks he knows it all, "Like you need to get over your mom dying. People die. Get over it. Just get over it."

We pulled into the driveway. I didn't turn off the engine. The lights were on in the entryway of the house, the turquoise glow visible, as Lucy looked out the window and then Theo pointed to our front porch. "She should be standing there. Right there, right now," he said. "And I'm mad."

I nodded, afraid that if I said anything, he would stop talking. But I was equally afraid of what he might say.

"Aren't you mad at Grandma?" he asked. "She should be visiting us. She should be watching Lucy at ballet, coming to games. She should see Henry graduate. Why are you never mad? Why do you always just seem OK, but never mad?"

He was talking louder.

"She was fun," he yelled at me. "She's the one who would take us to the park, the one who would hike with us when you said it was too hot. She took us to ride the roller coasters. She did. She should be visiting us now, she should know where we live, what we're like now. And she made you happy.

"You were happy," he said, much more quietly this time.

I wanted to disagree, to tell him that he didn't know everything, that I was fine, that I was happy. And as much as he was wrong, the truth was, and maybe still is, he also was right. I hadn't been mad. I'd been sad. Happy, too, over the years.

But he was right. It had been four years since my mom died. The details of what she sounded like and her expressions felt further away. As hard as it was, it's possible that for the first time, I let myself be angry with her, just for a while. To wonder what it would have been like to come home that night with a very angry Theo and have my mom there, maybe not on the porch, but there inside, playing Yahtzee with Lucy, cleaning the kitchen after dinner the way a mom knows you need, and waiting to sit with me, to rub my hand while I told her about my ride home with Theo.

While Henry and Luke both avoided talking about my mom, Theo's and Lucy's feelings were much louder.

With Lucy, it took four years to tell her the truth. Her brothers have always tried to protect her, and never told her. The question came from nowhere really. I picked Lucy up from her friend's house on my way home from work. It's a distance of twenty-three houses and two left turns. And she mentioned something from the house we rented when we moved to Cincinnati.

"I don't remember," I said.

"You have to," she said.

"But I don't."

I had no recollection. None. I tried to remember life there, the way it felt. But it was as if it had happened to someone else. And she was explaining it to me. I apologized and told her I didn't remember a lot from that summer, the summer after we drove from Phoenix to our new home in the Midwest. It was a few months after my mom died, from what I referred to then as a heart that stopped working to Lucy.

But today, I said, "I just had been so sad that summer after my mom died and that made it hard to remember things."

She looked at me, this time as a ten-year-old. So much more grown-up. Not suspicious. And not quite serious. Just matter-of-fact and honest.

"Tell me really," she said. "How did Grandma die?"

I didn't pause.

"Lucy, this will be hard to hear, to learn. But you are old enough now. So you should know. Remember how we learned that sometimes people who are very depressed commit suicide?"

She nodded, but looked at me the way she does when she can't quite read a sign without her glasses.

"That is what Grandma did," I said.

"But Grandma wasn't depressed," she said. She said it so honestly and with such disbelief. "She was always happy. She was always smiling when she came over. She was always ready to play or take us to the park."

We pulled into the driveway, but we didn't get out of the car.

"Lu, Grandma was happy. She loved all of us very much. But sometimes people who are sad seem happy. They can hide it sometimes," I said. "They can have good times, good parts of their lives. But it doesn't mean everything is good."

"How did she do it?" she asked.

"She jumped from something very high," I told her.

"Like a bridge?" she asked.

"Yes, but not a bridge. From the edge of the Grand Canyon."

Lucy looked sad and angry together. She didn't look at me, which is what she does when she isn't happy with me. She got out of the car, dashed up the stairs to her room, and slammed the door, no different really than if she'd fought with her brother over hitting too hard in a game of punch buggy. I knocked.

"Go away," she yelled. "You're a liar."

"You're right," I said. "I did lie. I did."

I walked downstairs to start dinner. I thought back to the evening when I needed to tell the kids and decided that Henry and Theo were old enough to know the truth. Luke and Lucy were not.

Then I went upstairs again. I knocked and then walked inside.

"What?" she said.

"I'm sorry, Lu. Not for lying because it was the right thing to tell you when you were five. But sorry that it happened," I said. "Sorry that you lost her. Sorry that we lost her."

She pushed me away, but she didn't yell.

She curled back into a ball, head on the pink unicorn Pillow Pet, one of the last gifts from my mom, a gift she feels too old for, yet too connected to to get rid of. I closed her door. I returned to the kitchen. I waited. Maybe twenty minutes later she walked down the stairs. Cheeks still wet. But no new tears. She wrapped her arms around me.

I wanted to say so many things. How much her grandma loved her. How my mom adored Lucy—from even before she was born. Her first granddaughter after six boys. How much I missed her. How much it hurt me. How I squinted and tried to figure out how many of those times that my mom stopped by our house with a beautiful smile and a hug, she wasn't happy. That she was just hiding and I missed it. So many damn times. But Lucy pulled me close. Her arms felt longer and stronger.

"I don't want you to do this," she said, not looking up at me.

"What? Do what?" I said.

"Promise me. Just promise you won't do this? What Grandma did. Please don't do it."

STANDING NEXT TO the canyon's edge with Lucy now felt both frightening and liberating. We had come to the canyon for a few days. And on this day it was so quiet and the sky was so blue that this time, walking toward the ledge felt safe. I needed Lucy to not just see that I was OK, but for her to feel it, that way you can feel something in your bones, which sounds stupid until you feel it and wish you knew a better way to describe it, but you don't.

We sat on the white quartz and looked off into everywhere and nowhere. We talked about my mom and her life. We talked about what her last day might have been like, and what she saw. And we sat and didn't talk at all.

Sitting there with Lucy helped to give me the clarity I needed. It gave me the feeling that I would live, that I wanted to live. It wasn't like it had been a few years before when it was enough to just not want to die. I wanted to be part of the world, I wanted a reason for being. It wasn't simply being here for John and my children, though that was part of it. It was a sort of faith I now felt, not in God, but in nature and people. This brought me to write.

I also felt I needed to tell the story my mom couldn't tell. But as I wrote, it seemed to be more about me than her, and maybe that was OK. I started with small parts at first, captions for photos of my mom that I shared on Facebook on her birthday turned into short essays almost, or more stream of consciousness writing if I'm honest with myself—and an editor would confirm! But then it became less about me. Others told me they had been there, they were there. It was both frightening and heartening, overwhelming and encouraging.

As I talked about it, I think I gave others space to talk about it.

Somehow I felt useful, that I could be helpful—it wasn't much, but it felt like something. Small posts turned a little longer and I felt ready, not just to tell the story of my mom, but maybe the story of me. I realized that maybe this wasn't just about her, that I needed to tell not just her story, but a daughter's story, mine. Our stories were so intertwined.

A friend who's an editor asked me if I might be ready to write about my mom for *USA Today*. It felt like an impossible task, to take everything that had been living in my head for the past years with my mom, the past decades with the sexual abuse, and how much would be too much to tell? My sister, at one point, told me it wasn't my story to tell, and maybe she was right. But I pushed ahead, and when I finished and my editor read it—and let's be honest, she had me rewrite it, and edited it again—it wasn't finished. Because one thing I learned is that writing and telling stories about suicide can have implications, and we wanted to be responsible in how we shared the story. We shared the story with a psychologist who's a suicidologist, Dr. April Foreman. I looked her up and she seemed nice enough, she had a funny photo of herself on Twitter and worked with veterans. She also works with the America Foundation for Suicide Prevention. After she read the story, she called me and thanked me for writing it. And then she asked, "What are you trying to say?"

That might be the worst thing to hear after you write something. Was it not obvious? It was a story about my mom.

"I wanted people to know, to tell a story of my mom, and maybe sharing that story would be enough," I said.

"But what else?" she asked. "What do you want to have happen?"

"For people to read it," I said, half-joking.

We talked for maybe an hour about my mom, about me, and she asked a question I hadn't thought about.

"What if there had been a barrier at the Grand Canyon?" she asked.

I laughed, to myself, of course, and asked where she lived.

"Have you ever been to the canyon?" I asked. "How practical would it be to put a barrier along 277 miles of a canyon, which is only one side?"

She told me that maybe the fence wouldn't go everywhere, maybe the park rangers have studied the issue, have data on where people have jumped, showing the most popular, if that's the right word to use.

"Was your mom's life worth a barrier?" she asked.

I sat quietly, unable to answer, or to fathom that someone

who just met me, who'd read something so intimate, would think I wouldn't want her alive, that I wouldn't do anything to have her back, that the guilt alone hadn't made me want to die. But my answer surprised me.

"No," I said.

She told me to not think of a barrier as a fence, but maybe a thick net of sorts such as what's at the Golden Gate Bridge. And suddenly I pictured my mom jumping, but not finding earth below her, instead landing in a net, like those at a circus, the kind I landed on and bounced when I took a trapeze class a few years ago. The image surprised me, cartoonlike in a way, seeing my mom bouncing up and back, and realizing that everything was a big mistake, and that instead of writing this, she and I are texting about everything and nothing, about how I planted iris bulbs last fall on her birthday, seventy for what would have been her seventieth birthday, a promise of spring, and of things I no longer could see, but had to believe were true.

"Laura," she said. "What do you think?"

"I don't know," I said.

I couldn't stop thinking about our conversation, about what could help. I would leave it for a while and then come back to the idea nights later, keeping me up at night thinking about what could be done, and how I wanted so desperately to make it happen right then. I remembered a sign I had seen at the top of a parking garage at my son's university that said, "Feeling hopeless? Remember, you matter. If you are considering harming yourself, call [a suicide help line number]."

What if there wasn't a barrier, but what if there had been

a sign, small and not intrusive to take away the beauty of the canyon? It was another what-if that entered my brain, a brain that had lived in what-ifs for the past years, the what-ifs about that one connection or encounter that would have changed the course just enough, that another one was possible, and then another and another.

I was the lucky recipient of such an encounter that kept me alive to another, and another, of no one entirely being the one or the reason I am here, but part of a larger net, of sorts, that kept me here.

Before my mother died, I always felt as if I couldn't ask for help. I felt that I operated without a net, that I was responsible for me, something that took hold during the years of sexual abuse. I was the one who could help myself survive.

But now, looking back, sometime after she died, I realized I needed the net, and one was there, though it would be impossible to plot out or see, or point to, but it existed nonetheless. It isn't one to replicate and when I try to dissect it, it's a blur of intersections, not a straight trajectory from depression to happiness. But one that exists. It is a faith I now have.

Can I trace what kept me here? It would be easy to say it was medicine and therapy, and family and friends and luck. Which tells a tiny part of a story, which isn't really much help. So what was it, and is it similar at all to what has worked for others? Could the similarities help others?

I thought about those things: the notes and words where I found comfort, walks to school with the children, people sharing their stories, all of it. And I thought about what happened when my story ran in *USA Today*,[2] of the people who read it and said it helped, but of one person in particular who told me it helped.

My sister.

She said the story captured our mom with love, and that she had been so afraid for me to write the story, that she was saving the memories and pieces of our mom, she was afraid that sharing them, talking about her, would somehow make her lose her again.

Two years later, my sister and I are growing closer. She tells me I can ask her anything. But I wonder if I am afraid of the answers, so we take it slow at first.

"Do you want me to look through photos," she asks, "to find anything for you?"

"Yes," I tell her, "if you think it will help."

We find a photo of our mom and dad, taken at an amusement park where they pushed their heads through a hole in a wood painting of the Muppets, making it look as if my parents are somehow in a hot-air balloon, and also are super fans of the Muppets. My dad looks like a 1970s movie star, his teeth and smile perfect, his black curly hair at least three inches high, his wire-framed sunglasses gray in the sun. My mom's red hair is curly and cut into a shag. She smiles in a way I somehow had forgotten, through all of this searching, that she used to do.

They both look so happy, actually happy, and I begin to wonder if they had been, but I can't see it anymore, I can only see the broken parts that now feel like confetti in our lives.

"Do you have memories of Mom being happy?" I ask my sister.

"Yes," she tells me.

"So do I," I say.

"So do you think it's true?" I ask.

"What?" my sister wants to know. "What is true?"

"That Mom was happy, that there were times when she was happy," I say.

"Yes," my sister says.

So, what is a childhood made up of? What do we remember—memories triggered by photos with enough details for our brains to fill in the rest? What will my children remember? The day I grabbed my purse and left for the airport, not intending to come back? The nights when I locked myself in the bathroom, crying until my eyes would barely open, snapping at the children for nothing? Or will they remember the mundane family dinners on a weeknight with everyone at the table sharing the funniest things that happened that day, the Saturday mornings on the sidelines, watching as they ran up a field or threw a pitch, the trips to the beach when we jumped waves together and dared each other to go deeper? Or is it all a blur that somehow amounts to something that mostly made them feel loved and that they belonged? That if they wanted, they could tell me things. That I was here, am here, and so grateful and glad for it. For them.

Notes

Chapter 2: A Growing Distance

1. Holly Hedegaard, Sally C. Curtin, and Margaret Warner, "Increase in Suicide Mortality in the United States, 1999–2018," Centers for Disease Control and Prevention, National Center for Health Statistics, no. 362 (April 2020), https://www.cdc.gov/nchs/products/databriefs/db362.htm.

Chapter 5: Learning to Understand Suicide

1. Gemma Richardson, "A History of Suicide Reporting in Canadian Newspapers, 1844–1990," *Canadian Journal of Communication* 40, no. 3 (2015): 425–45, https://doi.org/10.22230/cjc.2015v40n3a2902.

2. Centers for Disease Control and Prevention, "Suicide Contagion and the Reporting of Suicide: Recommendations from a National Workshop," *MMWR* 43, no. RR-6 (1994): 9–17, https://www.cdc.gov/mmwr/preview/mmwrhtml/00031539.htm.

3. "Recommendations for Reporting on Suicide," American Foundation for Suicide Prevention, 2012, https://

afsp.org/wp-content/uploads/2016/01
/recommendations.pdf.

4. Thomas Niederkrotenthaler et al., "Role of Media Reports in Completed and Prevented Suicide: Werther v. Papageno Effects," *The British Journal of Psychiatry* 197, no. 3 (2010): 234–43, https://doi.org/10.1192/bjp.bp.109.074633.

5. The White House, President Barack Obama, "Suicide Awareness Voices of Education," https://obamawhitehouse.archives.gov/champions/suicide-prevention/suicide-awareness-voices-of-education.

Chapter 7: Getting Better

1. Michael P. Ghiglieri and Thomas M. Myers, *Over the Edge: Death in Grand Canyon* (Flagstaff, AZ: Puma Press, 2012).

Chapter 10: My Mother's Daughter

1. Joan Didion, *The White Album* (Simon & Schuster, 1979).

Chapter 11: Moving Forward

1. Julie Cerel et al., "How Many People Are Exposed to Suicide? Not Six," *Suicide and Life-Threatening Behavior* 49, no. 2 (2019): 529–34, https://doi.org/10.1111/sltb.12450.

2. Laura Trujillo, "Stepping Back from the Edge," *USA Today,* November 28, 2018, https://www.usatoday.com/in-depth/news/investigations/surviving-suicide/2018/11/28/life-after-suicide-my-mom-killed-herself-grand-canyon-live/1527757002/.

Bibliography

Centers for Disease Control and Prevention. "Suicide Contagion and the Reporting of Suicide: Recommendations from a National Workshop." *MMWR* 43, no. RR-6 (1994): 9–17. https://www.cdc.gov/mmwr/preview/mmwrhtml/00031539.htm.

Cerel, Julie, Margaret M. Brown, Myfanwy Maple, Michael Singleton, Judy van de Venne, Melinda Moore, and Chris Flaherty. "How Many People Are Exposed to Suicide? Not Six." *Suicide and Life-Threatening Behavior* 49, no. 2 (2019): 529–34. https://doi.org/10.1111/sltb.12450.

Deutschman-Ruiz, Cindi. "Reporting on Suicide." Poynter. November 11, 2003. https://www.poynter.org/archive/2003/reporting-on-suicide/.

Didion, Joan. *The White Album*. Simon & Schuster, 1979.

Ghiglieri, Michael P., and Thomas M. Myers. *Over the Edge: Death in Grand Canyon*. Flagstaff, AZ: Puma Press, 2012.

Hedegaard, Holly, Sally C. Curtin, and Margaret Warner, "Increase in Suicide and Mortality in the United States, 1999–2018." Centers for Disease Control and Prevention,

National Center for Health Statistics, no. 362 (April 2020). https://www.cdc.gov/nchs/products/databriefs /db362.htm.

Niederkrotenthaler, Thomas, Martin Voracek, Arno Herberth, Benedikt Till, Markus Strauss, Elmar Etzersdorfer, Brigitte Eisenwort, and Gernot Sonneck. "Role of Media Reports in Completed and Prevented Suicide: Werther v. Papageno Effects." *The British Journal of Psychiatry* 197, no. 3 (2010): 234–43. https://doi.org/10.1192 /bjp.bp.109.074633.

Richardson, Gemma. "A History of Suicide Reporting in Canadian Newspaper, 1844–1990." *Canadian Journal of Communication* 40, no. 3 (2015): 425–45. https://doi .org/10.22230/cjc.2015v40n3a2902.

Trujillo, Laura. "Stepping Back from the Edge." *USA Today,* November 28, 2018. https://www.usatoday.com /in-depth/news/investigations/surviving-suicide /2018/11/28/life-after-suicide-my-mom-killed-herself -grand-canyon-live/1527757002/.

U.S. Department of Health & Human Services, Substance Abuse and Mental Health Services Administration. "Recommendations for Reporting on Suicide," SMA11-4640 (May 2011). https://store.samhsa.gov/sites/default /files/d7/priv/sma11-4640.pdf.

The White House, President Barack Obama. "Suicide Awareness Voices of Education." https://obamawhitehouse .archives.gov/champions/suicide-prevention/suicide -awareness-voices-of-education.

Resources

———

Resources in the United States

American Foundation for Suicide Prevention. Works to fund scientific research, educate the public about mental health and suicide prevention, advocate for public policies in mental health, and support survivors of suicide loss. Afsp.org.

National Suicide Prevention Lifeline: 1-800-273-8255; suicidepreventionlifeline.org or text TALK to 741741

SAVE, Suicide Awareness Voices of Education. A resource for those affected by suicide. Uses a public health model in suicide prevention with efforts on education and awareness. Save.org.

Acknowledgments

I BEGAN WRITING pieces of this book before I knew it would be a book. It started with texts to a friend from a baseball diamond next to the Ohio River watching my two youngest boys play the Saturday after my mom died, when life continued along and I tried to simply stay alive.

What started there continued on scraps of paper or Post-it notes, so that one day, I told myself, I would remember I wouldn't always feel this way. It continued in conversations with my best friend on our nightly walks with our two grumpy little dogs and in captions for Facebook or Instagram photos that turned into essays.

This would be a different book had I tried to write it just after my mom died, and a different one a few years later, and if I tried to write this today, I imagine it would change, too. But here it is, and I did it only because of my family and friends, and even strangers who reached out to me online after I posted bits about how I felt.

The tiniest of interactions sometimes got me to the next one, carried by friends with gestures they might not have even known were gestures. It exists because they confided their own loss, and shared in mine.

John Faherty was my husband and my love for half my life. This book, and me, wouldn't exist without him.

My sister, Lisa Lenstrohm, the only person in the world who shares the same love and happy memories of my mom, as well as the grief.

I'm so grateful that the brilliant and nurturing editor Kate Medina called me one December afternoon to ask if I was considering writing a book. She believed in my story, and more so, in my ability to tell it. When I was anxious that it wouldn't be good, she told me just to *write,* and let her worry about the rest. And so I did. I'm also indebted to her assistant, Noa Shapiro, who asked me questions that made my work better, and answered all mine, even those that seem silly now. Copy editors have been saving me for more than two decades, and the team at Random House is no different, and I am grateful for every last question and fix.

I was doubly fortunate when John's friend, the bestselling author Curtis Sittenfeld, was kind enough to talk me through the commitment of writing a book, and then connected me with Dorian Karchmar at William Morris Endeavor. Dorian got it. And she was the one who shepherded me through the process of taking a newspaper story and turning it into a book proposal. Because before it was a book, that's what it was.

And that story happened because Nicole Carroll, a friend and the editor of *USA Today,* texted to say: "Would you consider writing about your mom if I had Kelley Benham French edit it?"

And that is how I came to have the good fortune to spend an entire day in Kelley and her husband Tom's family room, sitting on the floor surrounded by notes, finding the arc of the story as their three girls played around us.

In between, and even before, so many people got me to a place where I could write this story.

I have been incredibly lucky to have good teachers who have looked after me and nurtured my writing, including my third-grade teacher, Mrs. Dow, and my favorite professor at Santa Clara University, Father Paul Soukup, SJ. I had newspaper editors who believed in me, made me rewrite and then rewrite again. Mike Arrieta-Walden and Inez Russel taught me the difference between an article and a story. Peter Bhatia and Sandra Rowe took a chance on me as a writer before I was ready, and Karina Bland and Krista Ramsey showed me the beauty of just sharing the truth, even if it doesn't always wrap up neatly.

I am thankful to my community of fierce and supportive women, who listened, asked questions that made me think, and inspired me with their own work. Especially to Maggie Gieseke and Diane Porter, to whom much of this book was written as a text. Both of you believed in me more than I believed in myself.

For Megan Finnerty, who has been a reminder of goodness and faith in the world, even when they are hard to find.

For the women who took over some mom roles: Nancy Frey, who was once my mom's best friend but in my adulthood became one of mine, and my dad's big sister, Valerie June, who has written me a letter each month since my mom died.

For the best of friends: Sara Fleury, who stood by me at the canyon, and for Hank Stuever for many things, but especially for taking one very teary phone call and reminding me I would be OK. And I am.

For my dad, who isn't much of a talker or storyteller himself, but who lovingly encouraged me to finish the book even though it made him uncomfortable.

I couldn't have written this book without the help from the National Park Service, in particular ranger Shannon Miller, and the rangers who were part of the thorough report that documented my mom's recovery.

Several other journalists helped tell this story, including Kelly McBride, Chris Davis, and photographer David Wallace..

I am grateful to Random House for investing in helping us all understand suicide—and its tentacles—a little better. I am also thankful for the Aspen Institute and Dr. Christine Moutier, the chief medical officer for the American Foundation for Suicide Prevention, for elevating the conversation. For Dan Reidenberg at Suicide Awareness Voices of Education, and April Foreman of the American Association of Suicidology.

There are incredible friends who have been here in various ways and whom I know I can always count on: the late Peter Farrell, the late Kyle Lawson, Chuck Rice, Amy B. Hunter, Emily Hartmann, William Philpott, Stephanie Bohn, Stephanie Arvin, Diane Jacobs, Rob Daumeyer, and Bill Goodykoontz.

I am also grateful to people who checked in on me or this book's progress at the exact right moment, even if they had no idea how much I needed it, and shared the needed encouragement. An extra thank you to Mike Link, Penny Walker, Tom Zoellner, and Miriam Hodesh.

I am lucky I had co-workers and leaders who acted just as excited as I was when I shared book updates, including Larry Magnesen, Teresa Tanner, Danielle Lewis, Amy Purcell, Sean Parker, and Melissa Stevens, and especially my work brothers, Kevin Quatman and Todd Musgrove.

And I am thankful for the families and friends of those who left too soon: Declan, Kimball, Darcy, and Gresh. I hope that everyone who is struggling with taking care of themselves and their mental health remembers to fight for it; you are worth it.

This book was written on the bleachers of Walnut Hills High School during lacrosse games, in the Mercantile Library, in the car while waiting for ballet class to end, and inside the coziest farmhouse north of Cincinnati belonging to the late Lynn Schiff.

Most of all, I am deeply grateful to my four children, Henry, Theo, Luke, and Lucy. You are each my beating heart, walking around, and helping me see the hope and future.

You cheered me on when I needed it, leaving me handwritten notes, telling me you were proud of me, ignoring the poster board covered in sticky notes that became a fixture in the dining room, and for understanding that it was going to be a long night when you saw me sitting on the heating vent with a Diet Coke, laptop shining, my headphones blasting The National.

And, last, thank you, Mom. I hope this story is as true as it can be. Once when I was much younger and writing fiction, you asked what the point of the story was. And you said, "If you aren't going to be helpful, don't waste your time." I hope this book would make you proud.

About the Author

LAURA TRUJILLO is a former reporter and editor for *The Cincinnati Enquirer, The Arizona Republic,* and *The Oregonian.* She now works in public relations and does advocacy work on behalf of suicide awareness. She lives with her family in Ohio.

About the Type

This book was set in Sabon, a typeface designed by the well-known German typographer Jan Tschichold (1902–74). Sabon's design is based upon the original letter forms of sixteenth-century French type designer Claude Garamond and was created specifically to be used for three sources: foundry type for hand composition, Linotype, and Monotype. Tschichold named his typeface for the famous Frankfurt typefounder Jacques Sabon (c. 1520–80).